CW01023896

2005-0

Away With the TIGERS

Paul Collingwood

TRAFFORD

USA ▪ Canada ▪ UK ▪ Ireland

© Copyright 2006 Paul Collingwood.
All rights reserved. No part of this publication may be reproduced, stored in a retrieval system, or transmitted, in any form or by any means, electronic, mechanical, photocopying, recording, or otherwise, without the written prior permission of the author.

Note for Librarians: A cataloguing record for this book is available from Library and Archives Canada at www.collectionscanada.ca/amicus/index-e.html
ISBN 1-4251-0050-3

Printed in Victoria, BC, Canada. Printed on paper with minimum 30% recycled fibre. Trafford's print shop runs on "green energy" from solar, wind and other environmentally-friendly power sources.

TRAFFORD
PUBLISHING™

Offices in Canada, USA, Ireland and UK
Book sales for North America and international:

Trafford Publishing, 6E–2333 Government St.,
Victoria, BC V8T 4P4 CANADA
phone 250 383 6864 (toll-free 1 888 232 4444)
fax 250 383 6804; email to orders@trafford.com
Book sales in Europe:

Trafford Publishing (UK) Limited, 9 Park End Street, 2nd Floor
Oxford, UK OX1 1HH UNITED KINGDOM
phone +44 (0)1865 722 113 (local rate 0845 230 9601)
facsimile +44 (0)1865 722 868; info.uk@trafford.com

Order online at:
trafford.com/06-1807

10 9 8 7 6 5 4 3 2

This book is dedicated to my father:

Edwin Joseph Collingwood

He took me to my first game in 1971, and religiously sent me Sportsmail clippings every week when I went away to college.

He died in 1994.

CONTENTS

	The Plan	11
1.	Damian – Hillsborough	17
2.	Steve – Molineux	23
3.	Chris – Home Park	29
4.	Pete – Selhurst Park	41
5.	Emma – Ricoh Arena	49
6.	Michael – Carrow Road	57
7.	Malcolm – St. Mary's Stadium	64
8.	Ben – Turf Moor	73
9.	Gary – Deepdale	80
10.	Dave C. – Madejski Stadium	91
11.	Tony – Loftus Road	99
12.	Stephen – Withdean Stadium	107
13.	Ray – Alexandra Stadium	114
14.	Dave L. – Elland Road	123
15.	Jon - Britannia Stadium	130
16.	Mike – Kenilworth Road	140
17.	Mick – The New Den	153
18.	Peter – Ninian Park	162
19.	Kevin – Walkers Stadium	170
20.	Lizzie – Portman Road	177
21.	Brian – Bramall Lane	185
22.	Dave C. (again) – The KC Stadium	190
23.	Michele & Hugh – Pride Park	198
24.	Nick – Vicarage Road	208
	Afterthoughts	210

A cramped changing room at Home Park.

Robert the mascot with McPhee, Woodhouse and Green.

My new friend, Stuart

The ITV Digital Stand at Preston

'Beam me up Scottie.' Tony's face says it all at Loftus Road

The Lead Singer—in full cry at Elland Road

Memorial to Sir Stanley at Stoke

A half empty Den on St. Valentine's Day

Gary Lineker overlooks the horrendous queues at the Walkers Stadium

Andrews' free kick whistles narrowly wide at Pride Park

THE PLAN

1st July 2005

My wife, Patsy, achieves a state of unnatural delirium when I inform her, that at the age of 42, I am finally going to hang up my boots and quit playing football on Saturday afternoons. She immediately begins to compile a mental list of laborious weekend DIY tasks to keep me occupied for the remainder of the decade, but I have neglected to mention, of course, what I am plotting to do instead.

I have a cunning plan, you see, based on Hull City's recent elevation into the Championship. This has thrown up the prospect of some mouth-watering away-days, and my bold intention, is to visit every single stadium in the division throughout the course of the season. Seven of our forthcoming opponents have moved into brand new accommodation within the last eleven years (Coventry are about to exchange contracts), and most of the remaining grounds have been extensively modified since the Taylor Report. Only Brighton have failed to upgrade. Instead, they have uniquely managed to downgrade, by moving out of the Goldstone Ground into the purpose built Withdean Stadium – purpose built for local athletics, unfortunately. Oh yes, and then there's Luton – I forgot about them.

This plan will commit me to twenty-three cracking matches, spanning the nation, over the course of nine months. It is a mighty tall order and many obstacles will be in the way: my long-suffering wife, my three demanding children, my full time teaching job, parents evenings, meetings, weddings, funerals (hopefully not), parties, illness, the weather, traffic jams, alien invasion…

But the publication of the fixture list in late June has given me cause
for optimism. My pre-booked family holiday to the Algarve has managed
to miss the away fixtures in August, and the long trek to Plymouth falls
nicely within my obscenely long teachers' summer break. But, the away
game at Preston on 1st November is the awkward one. Firstly, it is on
a Tuesday night; secondly it is over 200 miles from my Hertfordshire
home; and thirdly, but most importantly, it is Patsy's birthday. Still, I'll
cross that bridge when I come to it.

Undeniably, it will be a long and challenging road, but I shall not
be lonely, for I have drawn up a list of twenty-three companions to
accompany me to the fixtures (one to each game – I'm not bringing all
23 to every match). This was a surprisingly quick and easy process, as it
is now thirty-four and a half years since my first visit to Boothferry Park
(a 3-0 win over Charlton in 1971 on a snow-covered pitch). In that time, I
have persuaded a whole host of friends and family to attend meaningless
matches around the country; some have even come along willingly:
others had to be craftily convinced to look upon it as 'an experience'.
Many of the dilapidated grounds that we visited really did have to be
experienced to be believed: the crumbling weed-riddled terraces of
Rochdale's Spotland, for example, or the grit-covered speedway corners
of the Shay at Halifax. If I had managed to con people into visiting these
dumps, then the grand all-seated stadia of 2005 should see them beating
a path to my door.

The new luxuries of these state-of-the-art arenas are not the only
inspiration for my nationwide tour. A deep-seated hatred of teletext is
also to blame. In many ways, waiting for that score to flash up on page
318 (317 this season) can be a whole lot more nerve jangling than actually
attending the match. Whenever the relevant page appears, I panic, and
become seized by a rare form of dyslexia, which instantly jumbles up all
the letters and digits. I see fours, twos, and lots of zeros; there is always
a long list of goal scorers underneath one team, and the word 'Hull' is
in there, somewhere amongst the mix. The word blindness lasts barely
half a second before it all makes sense, but regardless of the outcome,
my pulse rate will not return to normal until well after full time.

I am still receiving therapy in relation to my worst teletext moment,
which occurred early in Peter Taylor's reign. The Tigers still had an outside

chance of making the play-offs, and a tough away fixture at Scunthorpe was going to be 'make or break'. At 4.15pm I finally plucked up the courage to flick on the text. City had just equalised, courtesy of Jamie Forrester. "YES!" Then it changed to 1-2 – Keates had scored. "YES! THE TIGERS ARE BACK! PLAY-OFFS, HERE WE COME!"

My frenzied circuits of the sitting room were cut short, though, when a correction was promptly displayed on screen. Scunthorpe 2-1 Hull City. Keates hadn't scored at all. He hadn't even scored an own goal. Wrong scorer and wrong team! How could they get it so wrong? Shortly afterwards, Scunthorpe scored a third. "NO! NO! NO! HOW CAN THIS BE? WE WERE 2-1 UP FIVE MINUTES AGO FOR GOD'S SAKE!"

Just to rub salt into my gaping wounds, two of Scunthorpe's goals were scored by Matt Sparrow. Oh, brilliant, a player named after the weediest bird in existence; I could just visualise the morning headlines; 'Sparrow Swoops to Tantalise Tigers', or 'Sparrow on Song to Tame Tigers'.

Now, it has to be said at this point: it is a fine nickname that my beloved side possesses, but in truth, it has been a huge burden over the years, as it just adds to the weight of expectation. Tigers are by nature, ferocious, unforgiving beasts, so journalists are unable to resist the opportunity to take the piss when we are shot down by one of God's meeker creatures. The knives are always out when we play Huddersfield, where defeat will normally lead to a burst of alliteration on the back pages: 'Terrific Terriers Tame Toothless Tigers'.

Not only did Sparrow's double satisfy the press, but it also put paid to our faint hopes of promotion, and consigned us to a nineteenth year of hurt. Only City could turn a 2-1 lead into a 3-1 defeat.

So, there will be no more teletext shocks for me, and no more gut-wrenching late equalisers being tapped out on Grandstand's vidi-printer either. Instead, I will witness all the drama first hand, in plush new surroundings (except for Brighton and Luton). Nothing will be left to the imagination. I will know exactly why and how we win, lose or draw. This will be a fascinating and entertaining voyage, where I can admire the 21st century architecture of purpose built stadia (except the Withdean), whilst enjoying the thrills and spills of Championship football. I just need to tell the wife.

COMPANION 1

Name: Damian Johnson
Birthplace: Hull
Relationship: School friend
Allegiance: Hull City

Relevant History

Choosing French as an 'A' level option was a big mistake. How was I to know that only two other people would make the same choice? Damian and Andy were both Premiership class linguists and I was Nationwide Conference. Traditionally, I had been the sort of student who survived by achieving the bare minimum, but in order to keep pace with this pair, the bare minimum would be set at an unacceptably high level; so much so, that it may even exceed my maximum. I was left with little choice: after six weeks of struggle, I said 'au revoir' to French, and took up the soft option of Sociology.

Damian and I were also members of another select trio within the sixth form, but our membership of this group brought us widespread ridicule. A keen biologist named Gary completed the intrepid threesome. Our collective crime was to repeatedly and deliberately attend football matches at Boothferry Park with blatant disregard regard for our own fragile teenage emotions. It was certainly character building stuff and we had to develop thick skins to deal with the communal piss taking back at school, which had become a Monday morning ritual. But the three of us continued to defiantly wear our City scarves around the premises, and we always looked forward to our study periods, when we could discuss at length the fortunes of our Saturday heroes.

The two Rugby League teams were riding high, and attendances at City were poor. We could bid each other farewell on a Friday afternoon therefore, with the confident prediction, "I'll see you at City tomorrow." We could wander freely around the barren terraces, so if Damian and Gary were in there, I would have no trouble finding them. It was probably a harder job to spot them in the pub later in the evening.

The unrestricted movement around Boothferry Park did at least mean that we could always get a decent view of City's valiant attempts to score. In the early days, we would start in Bunkers and then transfer to the 'Well' for 10p. Then we developed a preference for the North Stand (pre Grandways) and a switch to Kempton, where we could have a good old sing-song.

After leaving school, Damian and I would always meet up in the Haworth Arms on Christmas Eve. It was a guaranteed meeting place for Marist Old Boys, and the pub landlord was never aware that he was hosting our annual school reunion. It was an opportunity to gain an update on Damian's blossoming TV career with Look North and Grandstand, and he would take a similar interest, obviously, in my teaching exploits.

From 1994, though, I began to spend the festive season down south, and we lost touch – until – a chance meeting in the summer of 2001. Remarkably, it was not in the Haworth that we crossed paths; nor Hammonds, not even Boothferry Park. It was at Legoland Windsor. I was just wheeling my 3 year-old screaming son around a third circuit of the park in a vain attempt to induce his afternoon nap, when there in front of me is Damian, also on a relaxing, expensive family day out. I wasn't sure if he would recognise me (now that he's pals with Stubbsy, Lawro and Lineker) but he did, so we had a good chinwag and exchanged e-mails. We have kept in touch ever since. Naturally, about 90% of all correspondence relates directly to the Tigers.

VENUE 1 – HILLSBOROUGH

Sheffield Wednesday 1 Hull City 1

Tuesday 9th August 2005 – 7.45pm

My dream scheme very nearly gets derailed before it has even left the station. Damian had kindly secured the tickets for the first away fixture, but in true British comedy-farce style, he promptly tore them in half and threw them into the bin along with a number of ancient till receipts. Thankfully, the empty void in his wallet was discovered before the bin men did their weekly rounds, and the tickets were safely retrieved. Emergency repairs were carried out with a roll of sellotape, and the Sheffield Wednesday ticket office was contacted for reassurance of their validity.

I still harbour mild anxiety however, as I arrive at Damian's Sheffield home, in case an over-zealous steward declares them as pathetic forgeries. Gary (the third part of our sixth form Tiger trio) has made it across from Liverpool, and the two of them are already raring to go, so I have little time to voice my concerns. Gary drives, and Damian uses his expert knowledge of the local area to guide us into a bargain 50p car park at the new Owlerton Greyhound Stadium, which also incorporates shops and a casino. This money-spinning complex is the brainchild of Wednesday chairman, Dave Allen and it all helps to bring extra revenue to the club's coffers. Season ticket holders are allowed into the dog track for free on Tuesday nights, in return for gambling away the mortgage, I assume.

City's rapid rise from the ashes has caused attendances, both home and away, to snowball. My plan to find 23 different companions has never been a worry. To the contrary, it already appears that many additional followers will be attempting to gatecrash the scheme, and some of the more devout guests will be aiming to make more than the one allowable appearance. So it is, that Gary joins us, although his official match is not until November at Preston. We also arrange to meet Damian's brother, Frank, outside Hillsborough. Damian has got Frank's ticket, so of course, he won't get in without it: mind you, he might not get in with it either, the state it's in.

We begin the short walk to the ground, and like an awestruck seven year-old sampling his first ever match, I find myself getting unusually excited. I have been planning this for months, and the moment has finally arrived: the first of 23 consecutive away days. It is my first taste of Hillsborough as well. Back in the late seventies, my Dad had always reckoned that the Sheffield games were too dangerous, and he was probably right. Maybe, if we had ever reached an FA Cup semi final...

Damian hands us our taped up tickets. He's not actually done a very tidy job of repair, and I begin to wonder if he has even matched up the correct halves. They are made of very thin paper, and the print is a pale red: very unimaginative in design. It is quite easy to see how he mistook them for old shopping receipts when he was spring-cleaning his wallet. In contrast, the ticket for next Saturday's Wolves game is printed on good quality glossy card and is far more colourful. Could this be why it costs £10 more though?

Frank has been delayed, so Damian waits outside while Gary and I rush to our seats. The atmosphere is already electric and the West Stand is shaking with the ferocity of the pre-match chanting from over four thousand City followers. I calculate that it is wiser to take a leak now, rather than disturb my row mid-way through the half. The decision almost causes me to miss an early goal. Whilst in mid-tinkle, the roaring above my head reaches an excitable crescendo, followed by a booming "OOOOoooo..." When I reach my seat, Gary informs me that a goal-bound strike from Price was deflected wide by Elliott. I'm not sure whether to be relieved or disappointed. Damian and Frank then squeeze along the row, and I give them a detailed second hand description of Price's miss.

After the early excitement, I sit back and survey the area, and I am pleased with what I see. The sheer size of all four stands is staggering; they extend back so far. Each one is very much separate, but a number of seats have been added to the corner gaps, and the rooftops have been joined together at the front corners to give the impression of an enclosed arena.

Down on the pitch, the early signs are good. The Tigers are knocking the ball around tidily as they attack towards us, but it is Wednesday who make the breakthrough. Debutant, Leon Best, scores unchallenged from close range, but Damian is quick to remind me of what happened last December. The Owls scored first on that night too, but City had roared back for a memorable 4-2 win. Damian and Gary had not been able to fully relish that particular encounter, though, as they had been stuck right in the middle of a rather hostile section of Wednesday fans. Emotions were hard to control as events unfolded, but an overwhelming desire to stay alive had proved most helpful.

Unfazed by the early setback, City continue to press. Fagan then flicks a lovely ball into Barmby's path for the chance of a volley – time stands still as the whole stadium goes into a state of suspended animation. All minds flash back to last December, when Barmby scored twice (one, a thumping volley). Again, he meets the ball with great precision and it screams into the net. We hit the roof.

As we rise from our seats, Damian's mobile leaps out of his shirt pocket and disappears into the delirious crowd. He is oblivious at the time, and only realises after the celebrations have died down, and he spots some bloke three rows in front, holding it aloft, offering it to the nearest taker. Damian must have an honest face, for it is promptly handed back, no questions asked.

Meanwhile, Barmby has ridiculously been booked for yielding to the natural instinct of celebrating his goal with the fans. He didn't waste time; he didn't take his shirt off, and he didn't goad the Wednesday fans, so I can't see what the problem is. Didn't Leon Best get just as excited at the other end ten minutes ago? This is clearly another brainless refereeing directive from FIFA or the FA. "Players from the away team who are deemed to appear in any way happy following a successful attempt on goal, must be awarded a yellow card for attempted incitement of the home supporters." Don't quote me on that one, though.

For the rest of the first half, City take complete control, and it seems that only one team can win. Cort has a header cleared off the line and Elliott stings Lucas' fingers with a fierce volley. Our total superiority creates a deathly hush around the other three sides of the stadium. The diminishing Wednesday threat is highlighted by the crowd's desperate and laughable over reaction, when they believe that Myhill may have held onto the ball for more than the permissible six seconds. That's about as exciting as it gets for the Owls.

During the break, a number of people come and have a word with Damian, having recognised him from the telly. He takes it all in his stride and Gary accuses him of milking the attention. Gary then goes on to tell me of one classic misunderstanding when an elderly gentleman asked Damian for his autograph.

"My wife thinks you're wonderful," he enthused, but his face dropped when Damian handed him back the signed piece of paper. "Oh no. I thought you were George Alagiah."

Our domination continues in the second half, but we miss two golden opportunities to seal the win. First, Jason Price goes on a mazy dribble and rounds the keeper, before firing against the legs of a lone defender. Then, Elliott misses the sort of chance that he normally takes with his eyes closed. We fear that City will regret these misses, especially as in the last quarter we seem to lose the plot, and with it, the ball. Wednesday are now playing with it, and they themselves spurn some great chances to take all three points. Suddenly, I find myself settling for a share of the spoils.

It has been a pleasantly warm evening, but as the referee calls time on a 1-1 draw, the rain has set in, and this makes my drive out of Sheffield more problematic. I try to reverse Damian's complicated directions, but a combination of the rain, the dark and a series of one-way systems serve to get me hopelessly lost. It strikes me that this may become quite a common occurrence in the coming months; blindly driving round in circles in unfamiliar cities, hunting for stadiums and car parks, or just attempting to get out of town.

I eventually regain my bearings and pick up the A61 back towards Chesterfield, where my family are staying with my brother-in-law, a convenient base for the night, before returning south to psych myself up for the Wolves game. I wonder if we can extend our impressive two-match unbeaten Championship record.

COMPANION 2

Name: Steve Dyas
Birthplace: Hull
Relationship: School Friend
Allegiance: Hull City

Relevant History

The back of an overcrowded Transit van is not the safest or most luxurious way of travelling to away games, but it's the cheapest. Steve and I were eternally skint in the early eighties, so we relied heavily on this method for many of the closer fixtures. I can't remember who organised the trips, and I've no idea who drove, or whether they remained sober, or even if they held a license. I just know that there was no apparent limit to the number of people invited, and the only pre-requisite was to bring your own cushion.

An early season outing to Lincoln remains clear in my mind, as it was such a scorching hot day. The atmosphere in the back of the van would best be described as pungent: a stifling mix of hot air, over-powering body odour and beery farts. It was with great relief that we all piled out of the back doors at a country pub on the outskirts of Lincoln, but after four or five pints of cool lager in the warm sunshine, nobody had any great desire to carry on to the game. But, of course, we did – but we shouldn't have – it ended 0-0.

On the return journey, the van was even more jam-packed than on the way: I'm sure we had somehow picked up some extra passengers. It's a shame that an official from the Guinness Book of Records wasn't on hand to verify the record for the greatest number of drunken youths in the back of a Ford Transit. If we weren't breaking a record, we were surely breaking the law.

Steve is very passionate about the Tigers, and not much will stop him from getting to an important game. The famous Burnley game in 1984 when we needed a 3-0 win for promotion was no exception, and he was not going to be deterred by the minor inconvenience of having his leg in plaster, from his ankle to his arse. Again, we travelled in an overcrowded vehicle, but this time, Steve was afforded the privilege of a front seat place due to the complete immobility of his right peg.

Half way along the M62, the mystery driver asked Steve to take the wheel while he took off his coat. Then, literally seconds after returning control to the driver, the back tyre exploded and we careered all over the road before coming to a halt on the hard shoulder. Had the blow-out happened with Steve at the wheel, we may not have lived to tell the tale.

With a bit of trial and error, we somehow managed to change the tyre, but it was time-consuming and we were still not completely sure that it was going to stay on, so we proceeded with caution, reducing our speed by a good thirty miles per hour (seventy instead of a hundred).

The delay made us ten minutes late for the game, but our rush to the ground was further held up by 'hop along' Steve, who was now a real liability. There was no choice: we turned him into a horizontal position, tucked him under one arm, and ran. Other latecomers looked on in astonishment, probably believing that we were a bunch of ticketless hooligans attempting to use Steve as a battering ram to storm the Turf Moor gates. We made it onto the terraces just in time to see Brian Marwood celebrating the first goal. He notched another in the second half, but we couldn't force the third. It's the only time that I've come away from a match feeling gutted after a Tigers victory.

Allied to his Tigers passion, Steve also has a compulsion to follow England around the world. He has attended matches at all of the World Cups since 1982, and has been all over Europe, including many of the Eastern nations such as Moldova, Poland and Slovenia. He will be a good one to contact for travel arrangements when the Tigers get into the UEFA Cup, providing it doesn't involve Ford Transits.

VENUE 2 – MOLINEUX

Wolverhampton Wanderers 1 Hull City 0

Saturday 13th August 2005 – 3pm

A feeling of déjà vu overcomes me as I drive towards the centre of Wolverhampton: it is bucketing down with rain and I am lost. Stafford Road is the intended destination, but the basic map that I extracted from the Wolves website bears little resemblance to the streets before me. I reluctantly pull into a petrol station forecourt and flick through the town plans at the back of my trusty road atlas. From this I discover that Stafford Road extends beyond the ring road into the city centre itself.

The plan is to meet Steve in the 'Hogshead' in time to watch the opening premiership game of the season – Everton v Manchester United. With only five minutes to go before kick off, I finally spot the designated pub through my misty windows and park at the nearby civic centre.

The Hogshead is jam-packed with Wolves shirts but I spot a familiar figure on the far side, stationed in front of a large wide-screen TV; pint in one hand, burger in the other – unmistakably Steve. He has travelled down from Hull with Charlie, Phil, Ray and Fuzzy. Their dawn departure fashioned a conveniently early arrival time in the Black Country, so they have already completed a fruitful little pub-crawl. This is Steve's old stomping ground, having attended the Polytechnic here many moons ago, and he is not driving, so he intends to thoroughly enjoy himself in an alcohol-related type of way.

He introduces me to Kev, a friend from the Wolverhampton area, and we engage in conversation about Glenn Hoddle's credentials and whether Wolves can justify their billing as promotion favourites. Kev talks with a distinctive Wolverhampton twang, as do all of his mates: in fact, most of the pub does. It feels very much like I have gatecrashed some kind of 'Slade' convention.

It is actually a really efficiently run pub. If you are struggling to fight your way to the bar, a waiter or waitress appears magically by your side and takes your order; disappears for two minutes, then returns with a tray of drinks. Brilliant.

The caring service even extends to the gents toilets where a smartly dressed gentleman is posted to assist with the difficult operation of hand washing. His duties include: turning on the tap, squirting soap into your hands and tearing off a sheet of paper towelling. How would everyone have coped without him? Of course, nothing in this life comes free, and in return for his labour, punters are expected to throw some coins into a dish by the sink. This is all a new experience for me and I am slightly wary. I opt to use the cubicle in case he offers to shake my dick for me.

Half time arrives in the premiership clash, so the six of us head out into the driving rain. Just around the corner is Wolverhampton Polytechnic. Steve holds many fond memories of his time here, and I'm not surprised; its central location leaves it dangerously close to all of the town's best pubs, and Molineux is only a five-minute walk away. I ask Steve if he took these factors into consideration when finalising his decision for further studies, but apparently not – it was just the only place that would have him.

After another brief refreshment stop at the Ash Tree (known locally as the Ash Tray, due to its grotty interior and dense smoky atmosphere) we arrive at the ground – full of excitement, but dripping wet. The heavy precipitation continues to seriously precipitate beyond the three o'clock start, but Wolves seem to have no trouble adapting to the conditions and they take immediate control, with Kenny Miller proving a particular nuisance. It is no surprise when they take the lead with just 13 minutes gone, although Kevin Ellison does claim an assist by gift-wrapping the ball for Seol on the edge of the area. The Korean striker then lashes it across goal where Damien Delaney provides further assistance by deflecting it into the net.

A fair collection of puddles are now forming on the pitch, and even from our distant vantage point, we can clearly see great splashes of water spraying up from the turf with every challenge. Wolves' dominance is becoming a concern for a pessimistic couple behind me, and they concede that the best result we can now hope for is abandonment.

The home supporters, though, are in good spirits – so good in fact, that they spend most of the first half conducting a singing competition amongst themselves. After a brief lull, the South Bank taunts the opposite end with the challenge, "North Bank, North Bank, give us a song…"

To which, the North Bank reply, "You only sing when you're winning…"

Knowing when they are beaten, the South Bank resort to, "Who the fucking hell are you…"

This turns out to be a very good way of winding up the City fans. Not one insult has yet been hurled in our direction, and we are feeling extremely hurt and left out. It's not as if we need any help in the singing department; the lunatic just in front of us sees to that. He's up and down like the proverbial yo-yo, taking us through his full repertoire, flapping his arms with tremendous vigour to encourage vocal support. The look on his face is really quite frightening as he turns once more and bellows out, "Stand up, if you're Hull City…"

I find myself rising obediently from my seat for fear of the possible consequences. In fact, I'm sure I'd have still risen if he'd sung, "Stand up, if you love the Wolves…"

He reminds me very much of a former music teacher of mine.

Steve is familiar with the work of the 'lead singer,' having sighted him on several previous occasions, though he normally positions himself at the back of the stand and orchestrates proceedings from there. Just our luck that today, he has chosen to stand right in front of us, obscuring our view for the entire match. I get the feeling that we will be crossing paths again before the season is out.

Twenty-five minutes gone, and Myhill tips a Carl Cort header over the bar into the vibrant South Bank. The two end stands are identical in design, and with their black and gold colour schemes, they look uncannily like all-seated versions of Bunkers Hill. My overactive imagination then decides that we could be sitting in a redeveloped Boothferry Park. Not bad: it would be an impressive and acceptable home, but it's still not as good as the K.C.

Injuries to Andrews and McPhee lead to the introduction of Green and Elliott. The Tigers are suddenly transformed and some smart link-up play between Elliott and Ellison sets up Barmby for a poacher's strike, which is ruled offside. We all vehemently disagree and dutifully boo the officials as they break for half time.

The foul weather is a major disappointment. Back in June when the date for this fixture was first announced, my mind had conjured up images of players running to the touchline to rehydrate at every opportunity, watched by a t-shirt clad crowd, basking in the intense mid-August sunshine. So far today, it has felt more like mid-January, but when we return from the bar for the start of the second half, the dark clouds have miraculously vanished; the sun is beating down, and several of the overdressed people around me are now whingeing that it is too hot. I casually reach into the pocket of my waterproof, and become the envy of the sun-drenched Steve Bull Stand as I realise that I am the only person to have brought a pair of sunglasses.

The second half is more evenly contested. City's defence now look far more comfortable, and as 19 year-old Scott Wiseman's confidence grows, so Miller's influence fades. Elliott forces Michael Oakes into a couple of fine saves, but otherwise, there is little to shout about. It is our first defeat of the season, but Wolves are amongst the promotion favourites and we haven't been outclassed, so I retain my optimism for the season ahead.

So far, I have attended three matches. A crowd of over 22 000 joined me for the opener at the K.C. Stadium; nearly 30 000 were at Hillsborough, and 24 000 at Molineux. I almost need to pinch myself. Yes, this really is Hull City that I'm following. It has not been necessary to defect to one of the big Premiership outfits to experience this level of support. The Tigers are now playing in the fourth best attended league in Europe (ahead even of Serie A) and I'm loving every minute of it. I can't wait to get next week's holiday in Portugal out of the way so that I can get down to Devon to check out Home Park.

COMPANION 3

Name: Chris Coward
Birthplace: Hull
Relationship: Best mate's older brother
Allegiance: Hull City

Relevant History

Chris is sport mad. His main passions are probably football and racing, but he takes an interest in everything: cricket, rugby, golf, boxing, athletics – even the minority sports: table tennis, curling, tiddlywinks – you name it. He's not the sort of bloke you want to sit and watch 'A Question of Sport' with. He also possesses good organisational skills: sports tournaments, quiz nights, social events, etc. In 1994, he was presented with the opportunity to combine his powers of organisation with his love of sport. His brother Dave was getting married; Chris was Best Man, and as such, he was duty-bound to plan the stag night. He chose to centre it around Division Two's 'clash of the Titans'- Hull City v Chester.

He pulled a number of relevant strings at his place of work (the Hull Daily Mail) and – 'hey presto,' the Mail coincidentally became match sponsors for the day. Additional string pulling produced free passes for ten of his friends, a share of the pre-match buffet, and prime seats in the director's box. The festivities were to be rounded off by a quiet pub-crawl – the infamous 'Zooey Run' – a twelve-pub route along Beverley Road, from town to the Cross Keys.

Proceedings began early. We warmed up at lunchtime in the Three

Tuns with three pints, but we were all very careful not to eat much as we didn't want to spoil our free buffet. It would be an insult to the generous sponsors if we arrived without the obligatory raging hunger. At 1.30pm we ambled across Boothferry Road, and joined all the dignitaries in the reception area underneath the West Stand.

The bar was a bit of a disappointment; a small rickety table stacked with cans of Long Life, but at least we were allowed to help ourselves. The buffet had not yet been laid out, so we made do with several bowls of sweets that were thoughtfully spaced around the room as a nice little aperitif.

By 2.30 pm, the rumbling in our stomachs was clearly audible, and it was becoming obvious that the modest assortment of sweets was about as close as we were likely to get to a buffet. Etiquette suddenly went out of the window as we stuffed our pockets full of the left over strawberry creams to provide emergency rations for the long match ahead.

Thankfully, the promise of ringside seats was upheld, and we filtered into our positions, hopeful of a classic match to distract us from the malnutrition factor. The early signs were good. The pace of our headless chicken, Linton Brown, surprised the Chester defence and it wasn't long before he was racing clear to lob home the opener.

I have vivid memories of the match for another reason. My father had died four weeks previously, and I spent much of the game staring across at his old season ticket seat in Bunkers, convincing myself that he would be here in spirit, putting in a word with the 'top man upstairs' for a favourable result. Maybe he did. We won 2-0, with Dean Windass adding the second.

It didn't take us long to find a 'chippy' upon leaving the ground, and we ravenously lined our stomachs with a large cod and chips in readiness for the dozen pints ahead. Recollections of the final quarter of the crawl are somewhat sketchy, but I do remember appointing myself as official photographer, and this gave me an excellent excuse to stop drinking, in case I lost consciousness and lost the camera. I believe that Chris dragged Dave further along Beverley Road to the Parkstone and Rising Sun to make it fourteen stops in all. I bailed out at the Cross Keys and staggered across the road to my Mum's. She was still up. My bumbling attempts to act sober nearly pulled the wool over her eyes, but I blew it when I asked her to pass me the bin of tiscuits.

VENUE 3 – HOME PARK

Plymouth Argyle 0 Hull City 1

Saturday 27th August 2005 – 3pm

Unusually high numbers of Hull-folk are milling around Paddington Station, but it is unlikely that any of them will be Plymouth-bound. Instead, their eyes are scanning the departure board for the next Cardiff train in anticipation of their dream trip to the Millennium Stadium and the Powergen Challenge Cup Final. I feel no jealousy. I am a man on a mission, and I harbour equal feelings of excitement about the Tigers' third away outing of the campaign.

My hopes for a nice relaxing journey are quashed within seconds of taking my seat, though, as a scruffy young man plonks himself down beside me and proceeds to noisily chomp his way through the healthy breakfast-time option of a Big Mac. He polishes it off at alarming speed; yawns loudly several times; sniffs; grunts; coughs; yawns again; then leans across to ask if there is anything interesting in my newspaper. I begrudgingly hand it over, but within five minutes, he has skimmed through it, criminally ignoring the sports section.

He then turns to his horrendously boring-looking medical text, entitled, 'An Aid to the MRCP Paces' – not one that I've noticed on any best-seller lists. I try really hard to concentrate on my own book, but the fidgety 'medicine man' has the concentration of a goldfish, and after three or four aborted attempts to get to grips with the MRCP stuff, he gives up and asks me where he can get a coffee. I gesture towards the large 'BUFFET' sign right above our heads, with a gigantic red arrow underneath it, which points to the rear of the train: easy to miss I suppose, because there were no flashing lights on it. Before leaving he asks if I will watch his bag.

"Don't worry, there isn't a bomb in it!" he jokily announces to the whole carriage. I agree to take his word for it, although it would explain why he was so twitchy: still, anything for a bit of peace.

Within five minutes, he's back – without a drink. Either the buffet car was shut, or he'd taken a wrong turning: I didn't ask. God help the National Health Service if this guy is representative of the next generation of doctors.

We pull up at Reading Station and I sigh as Medicine Man remains firmly in his place. The two vacant seats opposite, however, are filled by a couple who are so thoroughly decked out in black and amber, that they look like they've just taken part in some kind of sponsored trolley-dash around the Hull City Shop. I immediately strike up a conversation with 'Dave and Trudy' and we happily spend the next two hours exchanging stories about past Tiger trips; or rather, Dave and I do – I sense that Trudy may be a reluctant convert and has married into this fanaticism, adopting the adage: 'if you can't beat them – join them'. She soon turns her attentions towards her crossword, but regrets this when Medicine Man insists on helping her with the clues.

Time flies by quickly, thanks to the light relief of Dave's Hull City anecdotes and we are soon at Newton Abbott, where I have arranged to meet Chris. He has once again used his powerful wangling skills to persuade his South Western newspaper group to sponsor a match of his choice, and with a world class wangle, he has somehow fixed up his 3 year-old son, Robert, as Hull City's mascot for the day.

In addition, we will wine and dine (booze and buffet) in a private box for the duration of the game. Sounds perfect, although the memory of the buffet at the Chester match, 11 years ago refuses to go away.

We arrive at the ground at 1 o'clock and are escorted like royalty to Box 16. This is, unfortunately, at the opposite end from the City fans, but no matter; a one-way window ensures that we are invisible to the Plymouth folk just outside, so we can still cheer, and pull faces at them at our leisure. Also in the box for the day's range of freebies, we have: Chris' wife, Angela and their children, Rachel and Robert; their friend, Fuzzy (who I met at the Wolves game); Mrs. Fuzzy (Nicola) and the two little Fuzzies (Isabel and Lydia). Fuzzy is actually called Paul: his nickname is derived from his surname, Furness. Lydia is only six months old and does not yet realise that she supports Hull City. She does however have a good pair of lungs on her, and it strikes me that this may not be the most relaxing atmosphere for watching a good game of football. It's more like a game of musical chairs in the cramped box: five adults, four children (all under the age of five) and a large pram.

Chris whisks Robert away to begin their sponsorship and mascot duties, leaving the rest of us to admire the view of Plymouth's smart little ground, which is three quarters complete in its all-seated reconstruction. The only stand left untouched is the one that we're in, and that will be flattened at the end of the season. Immediately below us lies the only stretch of terracing that I have seen so far this season, and up above are a couple of thousand extremely old wooden seats.

There are nearly two hours left until kick-off, but the efficient Home Park staff, ensure that we are not left twiddling our thumbs. Colin, an established member of the team, pops his head in and offers to take us all on a tour of the ground. We naturally jump at the chance, and after a peek in the changing rooms and a circuit of the pitch; we eventually end up in the away dugout to warm up Peter Taylor's seat.

With perfect timing, the City players then casually wander out to inspect the turf, so Fuzzy and I callously manipulate the children to engineer some photo opportunities.

Fuzzy has just taken a lovely snap of Isabel with Stuart Elliott when I leap in, virtually sitting on Stuart's lap, and mutter something about this one being for my nephew. He doesn't buy this for a second, but my embarrassing enthusiasm is tolerated and he happily poses for one more photo. Having outstayed our welcome, we are then politely, but firmly, ushered away, back to our little hide-away in Box 16.

Chris and little Robert return to the pitch at about 2.30pm. The main pre-match concern was whether the enormity of the occasion might cause Robert to freeze with fear, and retreat into his shell, but the exact opposite proves to be the case. After tiring of his kick-about with the Plymouth mascots, the young blond-haired Tiger toddles towards the City faithful in his over-sized black and amber kit, milking their applause with a swagger and a wave. Chris is touched by the warm reception that the fans offer, but they have in fact mistaken his son for Gareth Roberts, City's diminutive all-action captain of twenty years ago. Buoyed by the crowd's reaction, Robert returns to the centre-circle, and pushes over the official Plymouth mascot, Pilgrim Pete. This raises another rousing cheer from the Hull following who are delighted to see that Gareth has lost none of that midfield aggression.

Chris escorts Robert back up the tunnel, where they chance upon the referee's changing room. He can't resist it. A £20 note is hastily placed in Robert's tiny hand, and he is sent up to the referee, arm outstretched, primed with the question, "Are Hull City going to win?" Chris never actually told us if the gift was accepted.

With their obligations fulfilled, the boys return to the box to tuck in to the ample buffet. Waiters are regularly appearing at the door; they just can't do enough for us, although they stop short of changing Lydia's humming nappy. She is beginning to exercise the lungs, and appears to be paying very little attention to the match that has just got under way.

The Tigers begin brightly, and Delaney is unlucky to have a good goal chalked out for offside, but we suffer a major blow midway through the half, when Marc Joseph receives his marching orders. His offence was to have his stationary elbow head-butted by Bojan Djordjic. Pressure is heaped on the referee by the reaction of the crowd, and by the over-reaction of the tumbling Djordjic, who could do a fine job rolling the wicket at Lords. The incident confirms that Robert's bung has not paid off. In fact, the complete injustice of this decision suggests that we have been gazumped by the Plymouth mascot – the little sod.

Despite the setback, we comfortably hold out until half time, giving Peter Taylor a chance to take stock and reshuffle his pack. We too take stock, and discover that our glasses are empty, so we head for the bar. No sooner have we walked through the door, than the barman releases a loud cheer, snatches the black and amber jester's hat off Rachel's head, and merrily dances around the room singing City songs. We all agree that these Plymouth folk really are taking this, 'warm welcome' thing far too seriously, until we dicover that the excitable pint-puller is from Orchard Park – the same district of Hull as Chris. What a small world.

Taylor does indeed reshuffle things for the second half. Barmby and Price make way for Welch and France: Plymouth find it hard to break us down, and the ship has been steadied.

Another benefit of Box 16 is the television screen in the corner, which is tuned into the Challenge Cup Final. This is developing into quite a see-saw encounter and we find it increasingly hard to take our eyes off it as the conclusion draws near. At approximately 4.15pm, Paul Cooke breaks through the Leeds defence to score the cup-clinching try. At about 4.16pm, Stuart Elliott plants a sublime chip into the top corner of the net to give City the lead. Chris is still watching the replay of Cooke's try. He is gutted. After all the intricate planning and scheming that has preceded this game, he ends up missing the only goal. It is a cruel punishment for his brief moment of betrayal.

The final whistle goes in Cardiff, and I catch sight of my old school chum, Damian Johnson, giving an impartial BBC high five to John Kear, the Hull coach. I text him to advise greater restraint on national television, and to update him on the more important business of the City match.

Plymouth throw everything at us, which turns out to be very little. Our ten men easily see out the ninety minutes, and we hit the dizzy heights of 9th in the Championship. A third consecutive promotion beckons. I begin to dream, and suddenly I am spirited away to the cantilever stands of Old Trafford. Ronaldo is trying to beat Delaney with a few step-overs, but he fails miserably. He has still been unable to master the trick, despite exhaustively studying tapes of Chris Galvin and Leigh Jenkinson. His over-elaborate 2006 version just doesn't measure up to the Hull City maestros of the 70's and 80's. Elliott out jumps Ferdinand to head the goal that secures a Champions League birth. He cartwheels away to be congratulated by our new signing, Ronaldinho.

Loud jeers from outside the window help to snap me out of the hypnotic trance. The natives are restless and they are baying for the blood of their manager, Bobby Williamson. Perhaps I am getting slightly ahead of myself. We have just scraped a 1-0 against one of the division's poorer outfits and I'm already planning my European jaunts. Maybe I'll just settle for a play-off place.

COMPANION 4

Name: Peter Tisi
Birthplace: Plaistow, London
Relationship: College friend
Allegiance: West Ham United

Relevant History

Pete had been to one Hull City match before, in 1984, and because of the magnitude of the Tigers performance on that day, he has considered himself to be an honorary Hull City fan ever since. Indeed, anyone who was at Brisbane Road on that sunny November afternoon has the right to claim that title. City fans, Orient fans and neutrals alike will never forget the comeback of all comebacks that turned the season around and led to a promotion to the old Division Two.

It frightens me to think that I very nearly didn't go. Under normal circumstances, I would have been playing football myself on a Saturday afternoon for the college 2nd XI, but I'd had the 'good' fortune to dislocate a shoulder two weeks previously, so my Saturdays were my own until after Christmas. The only remaining hurdle, therefore, was to find a complete mug to accompany me to the game, but the prospect of rising from their slumber before mid-day on a Saturday would be a new concept for most students. It would require supernatural powers of persuasion to convince someone that it would be a worthwhile venture. Failing that, maybe bribery would work.

Orient's ground was not just down the road either. A trek right across the tube network of London would be necessary. We lived in Twickenham, which meant an initial bus ride to Richmond Tube Station at the end of the District Line (the green one). From there, a tedious journey under the capital had to be endured before changing at Mile End. Two more stops and we would ultimately reach the desired destination of Leyton Tube Station on the Central Line, (the red one). To be on the safe side it would mean setting off at about ten o'clock in the morning. Finding a companion was not going to be easy.

Each of the possible candidates could be sorted into three distinct categories:

a)   playing football; therefore ineligible
b)   not really that interested in football; therefore irrelevant
c)   pissed themselves laughing before I could finish the question

It really came down to the people in category 'c' as they were true football fans, hence their recognition of the hilarity of the situation. Pete fitted the bill perfectly. He was a good mate, and his love of West Ham's entertaining brand of football meant that he had been protected over the years from the harsh realities of the lower leagues. Such naivety could just lead him into my trap, so I popped the question. Once he had finished laughing, it emerged that his grandmother lived about ten minutes away from Orient's ground. Perfect. A deal was struck. He would come to the game so long as we could pop in there for tea and sandwiches before the match. Not quite the indulgent pub lunch that I had envisaged but I wasn't really in the strongest of bargaining positions, so Gran's it was.

My memories of that lunch are now vague but I often liken it to walking onto the set of Eastenders and having a 'nice cup of tea' at Pauline Fowler's. I do remember that his Gran was surprisingly knowledgeable about Orient's current league position and she even knew the names of some of their key players. A worrying thought briefly crossed my mind. Was there something that Pete hadn't told me? Was Gran going to be coming with us? I glanced nervously at the coat pegs, fully expecting to see an Orient scarf and hat hanging there in readiness. I was relieved to note the absence of any such red and white garments; just the standard array of grannie coats, scarves and brollies. With one eye on the clock and another on the door, we scoffed our cakes and knocked back the hot tea, scalding lips tongue and throat in the process. Job done, we left in good time (before Dot Cotton popped in) and began the short walk to the ground for the big match.

By 3.30pm my world had caved in. Orient had stormed into a 3-0 lead and were carving open the City defence at will. I turned to Pete to apologise. He was pissing himself laughing. I really should have come alone. Until now, Pete had possessed no hard evidence to back up his lowly view of Hull City Football Club. But now I had helped to provide it. I had foolishly invited him along to witness first hand how painfully poor third division football could be. And he would tell. He would tell everyone. The unsuccessful candidates back at college would all be informed that their mocking response to my offer had been fully justified. But then, on the stroke of half time, the Orient keeper provided a glimmer of hope when he obligingly dropped Billy Askew's corner into his own net. Game on!

The interval was spent trying to convince Pete that this fluke goal would be the turning point of the match. He was fascinated by my blind optimism. I had to confess that I hadn't actually seen City over-turn a 3-0 deficit before and, yes, they were woeful today, and no, I hadn't spotted any flying pigs recently. Still, I remained upbeat and I heartily cheered the Tigers back onto the pitch as they prepared to lay siege to the Orient goal.

My misguided resolve was finally broken twenty minutes later when Orient scored their fourth. It has to be the most deflating and humiliating experience in football, to witness the other three quarters of the stadium erupt in euphoric delight as the opposition hit the net. All you can do is stand and watch in stunned silence. It appears that as well as cheering, they are also laughing. Laughing with mighty gusto, pointing fingers in your direction, wondering why on God's Earth you would want to waste your weekend travelling two hundred miles to watch this pathetic shower. The humiliation then turns to anger and invariably manifests itself with chants of, "You're gonna get your fucking heads kicked in!"

And so it was, as most of Brisbane Road celebrated an unassailable 4-1 lead. The name of the scorer was announced over the P.A. and another rousing cheer rang around the ground. Chants of "Come on you O's" echoed in my ears. Dumbstruck, I consoled myself with the crumb of comfort that they had a totally crap nickname. "The O's," I thought.

"What unimaginative moron came up with that one? It would be like calling Plymouth Argyle the A's, or Luton Town the T's, or Hull City the C's." Mind you, at that particular stage of the game, I think plenty of our fans *were* calling City the C's - useless C's.

My thoughts began to turn towards the journey home. Several other fans had also hoped for an early release from the suffering, but it soon became apparent that for safety reasons, or maybe just because they thought it was funny, the police were going to keep us penned in until well after the final whistle.

To amuse ourselves for the final twenty minutes, Pete and I participated in a little game of plane spotting. The skies were clear and a steady stream of jets made their way over the ground on the approach to Stansted. As our college campus lay right beneath the Heathrow flight path, we had become quite accomplished at knowing our Boeings from our Tri-Star's. Having classified the model of plane we would then compete to spot the country of origin via the markings on the tail. Oh, hours of fun! I'm sorry, but as things stood, it was the best that we could do.

While my eyes were raised to the heavens, I decided that a little prayer might not go amiss in an attempt to improve the situation down on terra firma. And wow! I have to say, the response was pretty immediate even by God's own high standards. From nowhere, the Tigers banged in two goals and there were still fifteen minutes left. The game opened up and chances were being created at both ends. We had a lucky escape when Orient hit the bar, but then, with five minutes remaining, another prayer was answered. I'm not sure which one because I'd said so many. A hopeful ball had been punted into the O's box and had struck a defender's arm. Penalty...surely. All Tigers eyes scoured the pitch for the referee. He was pointing at the spot!

Stan was the man. Stan McEwan, the man who had been known to break the net with 25-yard free kicks. From 12 yards he could break the goalkeeper, and each keeper in the division knew it. The generally accepted routine was that Stanley would thump it with great ferocity straight down the middle and the keeper, if he knew what was good for him, would dive as far away as possible. Some older and wiser guardians of the sticks had been known to make it wide of the penalty area.

Yet, despite his exemplary record from the spot, I was sure he was going to miss. It was all too good to be true. How could we possibly snatch a 4-4 draw? All the City fans were sucked down the terraces towards the back of the goal, ready for the wild celebrations. No pressure Stan. It crossed my mind as the referee gave him the nod that my dodgy shoulder could get quite a battering should the kick be successful. But it was too late. I was hemmed in and Stanley was on his way. Chalk dust flew up as McEwan scuffed his shot, but the diligent Orient keeper had done his homework and he dived well wide of the goal. The ball bobbled into the net and my shoulder winced.

That was it as far as I was concerned. We'd got out of jail and nicked a point. All we needed now was for the ref to blow his whistle and we could all go home happy. But there was to be one final twist. As the game entered stoppage time, the Tigers cleared their lines for what they hoped would be the final time. Ear-piercing whistles blew out across the pitch towards the referee, willing him to end the contest. Maybe his watch had stopped. We blew harder. Maybe he'd been enjoying the free-scoring game so much he'd just clean forgotten about the time. Yes, he was definitely relying on the City contingent for a reminder. We kept blowing.

The whistling then turned suddenly to crazed screams of encouragement, as Steve Massey appeared to have broken clear of the Orient defence. Just for a second we all dreamt the impossible, but then his tired legs failed to get the ball fully under control and he was forced out wide. Massey clearly wasn't as clever as we thought, however, for instead of sensibly heading for the corner flag to see out time, he whipped in a low cross which picked out Andy Flounders, the only City player to have kept up with play. Flounders clipped it first time across the keeper into the bottom corner of the net.

We went so deliriously mental behind the goal that I even allowed my arm out of its sling to join in the celebrations. Pete meanwhile, was truly caught up in the euphoria as he danced and sang, whilst hugging several sweaty strangers from East Yorkshire. The wild scenes were duly granted an extension by way of the referee's final whistle and nobody gave a toss how long the police kept us penned in.

The journey home seemed to go very quickly as I relived every moment of the game and read the programme several times from cover to cover. On our eventual return, I headed straight for the college bar to toast the triumphant Tigers and to seek out vulnerable, traumatised

Orient fans.

Back home, the excitement of listening to events unfold on Radio Humberside had proved too much for my cousin, Hugh, and his wife Michele. She went into labour that evening and gave birth to a son, Martin. I'd have called him Stanley myself.

VENUE 4 – SELHURST PARK

Crystal Palace 2 Hull City 0

Saturday 10th September 2005 – 3pm

Pete's mate (a crystal Palace fan) advises us to disembark at Thornton Heath Station and aim for the Prince George. He assures us that the away fans always gather there in abundance. We are convinced that he is leading us into a trap, but we still follow his instructions, for lack of any viable alternatives.

The pub is a short walk from the station, and we find it easily, but distinctly hostile vibes are radiating from within, and loud, aggressive football chants are rattling the windows. We approach with trepidation, awaiting the ambush, but are pleasantly surprised to discover that the raucous war-cries belong to just three Hull City fans who are already well into their alcohol-fuelled stride. The vast majority of the punters are dressed in City shirts, but have distanced themselves from the crazy-gang, especially as the ringleader is now dancing around with a cabbage on his head. We too disown him and settle down at the opposite end of the bar, next to a large stone fireplace.

Within minutes, my two cousins, Michael and Stephen, wander in from the High Street. They actually have no right whatsoever to be here. Both were born in South Africa, and were raised in Hampshire, but in true bandwagon style, have adopted the blossoming Tigers as their own, and are now taking in a selection of the southern fixtures. Funny, it only seems like yesterday that they were mercilessly taking the piss out of my blinkered allegiance to that useless third division team. How times change.

Our seats are uncomfortably close to the gents, and it's not long before the 'cabbage man' passes through on his way to the urinals, jauntily swinging a posh silver-topped cane. In the absence of any discernible limp, I assume this to be some kind of fashion statement, 'a la' Chris Eubank, but instead of the dapper suit, he is sporting a replica City shirt and faded jeans.

As he exits the men's room, I can't resist asking him about the significance of the cabbage. He explains, that in the wake of England's recent defeat in Northern Ireland, he would "rather have a cabbage than a Swede." I have unwittingly opened up a can of worms here, and he launches into a tirade about the incompetence of Mr Eriksson. We can't shut him up. I attempt to send him on his way by dropping the standard subtle hints, like yawning and checking my watch, but he's having none of it. He draws up a stool and settles in for the long haul. We only wanted to know about the cabbage, but we get the life story.

He moved to Hull from London when he was seventeen, which explains the faded QPR tattoo on his left forearm. A far more prominent Tigers tattoo is evident on the right arm. He goes on to tell us about his fierce patriotism and his vocational following of England, all over Europe. Apparently, a range of England tattoos adorn various parts of his body, but thankfully, he is not inclined to prove this to us.

I glance despairingly across to his two chanting chums, praying that they will intervene and drag him away, but they've scarpered. Plainly, the cabbage man has travelled alone and he had just latched onto them: now he has latched onto us.

Telepathically, the four of us speedily drain our glasses and rise to leave, trusting that the cabbage man will not tag along. Happily, he doesn't. He prefers instead to seek out some more unsuspecting souls, continuing his quest to put the footballing world to rights.

As luck would have it, our premature exodus from the pub does us a favour. We arrive at Selhurst Park to find ridiculously long queues tailing back from the turnstiles. Painfully slow security checks are in progress, and each supporter is receiving a thorough frisking: unnecessarily thorough in the case of the attractive girl in front of us.

Pete and I are accepted as decent law-abiding citizens, but my cousins are made to sweat. Stephen's five o'clock shadow is strengthening my Mum's argument that leaving the house without a shave can dramatically increase your chances of being arrested. She has a bee in her bonnet about this, and recently introduced me to a friend of hers in Tesco's in the style of Hyacinth Bucket, with the line, "This is my son, Paul; he normally gets a shave."

Cheers Mum.

Stephen eventually convinces the police that his small rucksack does not contain swag from an overnight job on the local housing estate, and we just make it in time for kick off.

Once again, City begin brightly, but their recent obsession with the woodwork resumes on twenty three minutes when Barmby strikes the underside of the bar. (The previous Saturday, at home to Leicester, we had hit the goal frame on four separate occasions). Palace offer no real threat in the first quarter, but then Tom Soares - one of Taylor's under 21 prodigies – gathers the ball in midfield, and without warning, goes for the jugular; taking on the entire City defence. Our back four all rashly dive in like novice lemmings, but Soares commendably hurdles all attempts to take him out and eventually reaches the by-line. He pulls it back for Clinton Morrison, the Prodigal Son, to tap in.

Andy Johnson is having a quiet game, except for one flash of genius, when he does a Soares, and weaves through seven City players. A perfectly timed tackle from Roland Edge is required to prevent him from going all the way. This leads to the umpteenth chorus of,

"You'll never play for England."

The singing is again a feature of the match. I have detected over the last four games that songs are no longer violently provocative: the provocation is now more humorous. There is never a shortage of nutters in the City end willing to lead the vocals, and today, a rather large chap in a pale pink polo shirt is particularly prominent. It may actually have been a white shirt that got washed with a pair of red socks, but nonetheless, he soon regrets wearing it, because it sets him up as an obvious and easy target for the Palace fans.

They identify him immediately, and then ruthlessly take him out by bombarding him with insulting, but witty, laser-guided songs.

"You fat bastard, you fat bastard…"

"Who's the wanker in the pink?"

"Does he wear his mother's dress?"

He takes a bow to the Eagles contingent, and then sits down – a broken man.

The interval arrives, and as usual, the half-time entertainment fails to live up to its name. Firstly, we have an imaginative competition, named: 'On me Shed Son,' where a lucky programme winner attempts to chip two out of three footballs into a roofless shed. The prize is a £2500 Wickes kitchen, but unless David Beckham is sitting in the stands, clutching the relevant programme, the kitchen will not be leaving the showroom. Yet, human nature dictates that if there is a big enough carrot dangling at the end of the stick, we are willingly prepared to make a complete dick of ourselves in front of twenty thousand people. The sucker who finally emerges to attempt the impossible, fails to even hit the shed. A barn door wouldn't have been troubled either.

Next, we have the Palace Crystals: a bunch of 15 year-old schoolgirl cheerleaders. Pete is particularly interested in this act, not because he is a pervert, but because his friend's daughter is in the team. That's the same friend who recommended the Prince George. Pete is obliged to watch so that he can pay her great compliments on the way she waved her pom-poms.

Talking of Poms, the fifth test against the Aussies is then displayed on the big screen above the Croydon Advertiser Family Stand. This is even less entertaining than the cheerleaders. Australia are 212 for 1 and England's chances of regaining the Ashes are looking slim. Rain is our best hope.

The torturous cricket is turned off as the players take the field for the second half. The 'wanker in the pink' fails to return to his original seat. He has either moved or swapped shirts with someone. This is noticed in the Holmesdale Stand and they won't let him get away with it.

"Where's the wanker in the pink?" they sing.

Neither side are able to create many clear-cut opportunities after the break, but as we near full time, City are placing the Palace defence under increasing pressure with a succession of crosses and corners. I sense a late equaliser, but the dormant Andy Johnson senses a breakaway clincher.

He erupts into life on 89 minutes by stealing the ball off Welch, and sprinting towards goal like a whippet. His England credentials are displayed for all to see as he clinically fires past the stranded Myhill. The trademark gliding eagle celebration follows, but to his credit, he totally ignores the Tigers fans that have been taunting him all afternoon.

The defences in the Championship are far more miserly, and today's game has underlined the need to 'take your chances.' The depressing atmosphere is further dampened as we file out: the skies darken and the heavens open. Pete, Stephen and I hastily reach for the waterproofs that we have been dragging around with us all day, but Michael's thin t-shirt is offering little protection and he gets a thorough soaking. At least the rain will be more than welcome down the road, at the Oval, where the Aussies will be prevented from building up a substantial first innings lead.

We reach the back of the Holmesdale Stand, and immediately dip our heads as we spy a dripping wet Cabbage Man, 'singing in the rain' at high volume – on his own. We need no further evidence to confirm our belief that the man is indeed a sandwich short of a picnic. We have a 3 to 1 agreement that only a complete fruitcake would come out in weather like this without a coat. Michael is the only dissenter.

The police weigh up our cabbage-loving friend as a harmless eccentric, and with a distinct lack of stubble on his face, he is unlikely to face arrest today, whatever he does.

So, it's a damp and dismal end to the day, and Pete does not magically bring the Tigers luck after all. I felt confident that when Johnson made it 2-0 in the 89th minute, we would still storm back for a 3-2 win. Maybe all his psychic energies were focused on the cricket, where England incredibly achieved a first innings lead before batting out the final day for an Ashes clinching draw. As Jimmy Greaves would say, "It's a funny old game."

COMPANION 5

Name:	Emma Lewis
Birthplace:	St. Albans
Relationship:	Work Colleague
Allegiance:	Everton

Relevant History

When nailing their colours to the mast, most normal people are drawn towards the side from their home town. Others prefer the fair-weather approach, and adopt the club that is sitting at the top of the league. Some, however, follow less conventional criteria. Take Emma, for example. In her formative years, she swore allegiance to Everton. This was not down to any family connections with the City of Liverpool; she was born and bred in St. Albans. Neither was it down to any lofty Evertonian league placings. No, quite simply, she chose Everton because it begins with the letter E, and so does Emma. She counts her blessings daily that she doesn't live in Scotland or she may well have plumped for East Stirling, perennially bottom of the pile.

Her peculiar decision-making process is understandable, even forgivable; we have all made regrettable choices at the age of seven that now cause us to chuckle with embarrassment. I, myself, placed a Leeds United kit at the top of my 1972 list to Santa, garter tabs and all. (Ho, ho, ho). I am able to laugh now, just. But, the most remarkable thing about Emma's early choice is her admirable determination to stick by the Toffeemen – even throughout those difficult self-conscious teen years, where any self-respecting youth would surely have re-evaluated their image, ditched Everton, and gone along with the crowd.

Fair play to her, though: having survived the calling of Spurs, Arsenal, Chelsea and even Watford, she reached the age of 18, and packed her bags for teacher training college in the north-west – Crewe, to be precise – a suspiciously convenient base for Goodison Park.

Her loyalty has also been unaffected by her status as Everton's unluckiest supporter. In the past twenty years, she has personally cheered on the Toffeemen on 27 occasions, but amazingly, has only seen them win once: an appalling record. If Everton Football Club ever become aware of this curse, they will surely employ heavy-handed methods to ensure that she is banned from all future matches.

The bad fortune appears set to continue; in fact it is becoming more severe. Her boyfriend arranged her last outing, as a romantic surprise: two tickets for Highbury to see them take on Arsenal. He plainly thought that he could worm his way deep into her affections with this thoughtful gesture, but the Gunners thrashed them 7-1. Emma and Everton were completely humiliated, especially as she had to sit just a few seats away from the Arsenal fans, and most of their insulting songs and remarks were aimed at her – the only female in the Everton section. She has never forgiven him.

She really should have got the message by now and found herself another team. The curse *does* seem to be restricted to Everton. Her boyfriend follows Watford, and he is convinced that Emma has the opposite effect on their fortunes. He is constantly trying to coax her along to Vicarage Road, as they always seem to win when she visits. What effect will she have on the Tigers?

VENUE 5 – THE RICOH ARENA

Coventry City 0 Hull City 2

Saturday 24th September 2005 – 3pm

The brand new Ricoh Arena is situated to the north of Coventry and is easily accessible from Junction 3 of the M6. We experience no navigational anxieties therefore, and even parking is a breeze. A swarm of efficient attendants in luminous jackets guide us to a place, which turns out to be in the middle of a large industrial estate. The businesses here have kindly surrendered their car parks for the day, though not without financial gain. No sooner have I manoeuvred into my slot, than I find myself handing a fiver through the window. Emma informs me that a similar arrangement operates outside Goodison Park, except on Merseyside, the attendants take the form of hooded youths who kindly provide the added guarantee that they will not brick your windows.

We lose our bearings upon reaching the stadium as the letters above the turnstiles do not appear to correspond with the information on our tickets. We seek Block 11, and Vomitory 39, whatever that is (sick-bay possibly). Typically, I choose to ask the world's most stupid steward for advice.

"Excuse me, where do we go for the Hull end?" I enquire.

He appears perplexed. It's a common problem. It's *that* word, 'Hull.' It sounds too much like the word 'Ugh.' People just think that you're grunting at them. Whenever anybody asks where I'm from, I always have to repeat the answer. Maybe we should call the city Kingston; then the only confusion would be the distinction between Kingston-upon-Hull, Kingston-upon-Thames and Kingston, Jamaica. Also, it wouldn't rhyme with dull any more, and ignorant outsiders might just give the place a chance. Undaunted, I try again.

"The Hull City fans. Where do we go?"

"This turnstile is for Coventry fans," he replies.

"Yes, I know! We want to be with the other team; the opposition; the away side; the team that is not Coventry. Ugh City!"

Finally, a little light seems to go on. He raises an arm and points to his right.

After two minutes of walking in the given direction, we notice that most of the black and amber shirts are walking the other way. We carry on regardless, safe in the knowledge that the stadium is circular, and we will get there eventually. Half way around the circumnavigation, we come across an interesting little feature. Built into the fabric of the arena's outer concrete casing, there are a series of smaller special walls, each dedicated to famous players and managers of the past. Fans have paid great sums to have their names engraved into a brick of their choice. The gold script was more costly than the black, which is a bit of a con, because the gold reflects the sunlight and is impossible to read.

The first section that we pass is entitled, 'The Brian Kilcline Wall.' I'm not patient enough to stop and count, but there must be over a thousand bricks for each player. Next up, is the 'Steve Ogrizovic Wall,' followed by John Sillett and Ernie Hunt. Then unbelievably, comes the 'Jimmy Hill Wall.' Even more unbelievably, it is just as large as the others, and it's completely full. I can only assume that this must have been the last wall to be finished, and that the names contained within, represent the unfortunate fans that didn't get their act together, and were forced to accept what was left.

Our derogatory remarks seem to offend an eves-dropping steward nearby. He is brighter than the last one and is able to explain that Mr. Hill is in fact a well-respected member of the Coventry community. In that case, the famous phrase must work in reverse, and anyone refusing to talk to Jimmy, must have to send him *out* of Coventry.

Once inside the ground, it is obvious that there are many similarities between the Ricoh Arena and my new bathroom: it's not finished yet, but we've moved in anyway. Beneath the stand, in the bar area, a lot of bare breezeblock and scaffolding are visible, but the view from our seats behind the goal in the Jewson Stand is mightily impressive. The September sun is shining brightly and the new pitch is in pristine condition. This idyllic Saturday afternoon scene, though, disguises the fact that hundreds of builders, officials and ground staff have turned into quivering wrecks after working round the clock to be ready for the start of the season. The programme notes reveal that the team of groundsmen (all four of them) were given only three days to work on the pitch for the opening fixture. They are not helped by the fact that it grows half an inch each day, so if they cut it in the morning, it is back again by the evening: a bit like George Best's beard.

During the early exchanges, I explain to Emma that Boaz Myhill is one of the best keepers in the division. Within seconds, he has let a speculative effort from Michael Doyle squirm through his fingers. It trickles narrowly wide of the post: he had it covered!!

City soon suss that Coventry's prime tactic is to hoof a long ball to the powerful Dele Adebola, but Delaney and Cort double up and keep him under wraps. The Tigers soon begin to create chances of their own. Barmby floats a delightful chip over the Coventry defence to play in Chris Brown for a golden opportunity to open his account, but Stephen Bywater's legs foil the Sunderland loanee. This miss does not prove costly, though, because a minute later we are in the lead, courtesy of a deflected cross. I can't make out who has scored, so I look around for the scoreboard. There isn't one. The public address system fails to provide any clues as it echoes out something totally unfathomable. I've heard clearer announcements at Paragon Station. The importance of communication with the crowd seems to have been entirely overlooked in the mad panic to get everything ready. Still, at least the grass looks nice.

Brown nearly scores again – twice. Firstly, with his back to goal, he hooks the ball marginally over, and then, he curls a great shot around the keeper, but it clips the outside of the post. He could have had a hat-trick but it's obviously not his day. Myhill then pulls off one of his customary blinding saves from Gary McSheffrey and I get edgy as half time approaches. I look around for the clock: there isn't one.

The ref blows for the break and the neutral Emma agrees that Coventry have got off lightly. The players march off for their half time cup of tea and the sprinklers suddenly pop up to water the newly bedded turf. It seems ludicrous that on such a glorious day, they should want to shower the pitch with artificial rain to create a zippy-slippy surface. Surely, this would not suit the long balls to Adebola, which would now just skid through to Myhill, but the pitch appears to be the number one priority, and even the school children involved in the half time penalty shoot-out are not exempt from a good soaking.

Despite all the missing accessories, I am impressed with the new 32 000 all-seater stadium. Today, there are 21 000 inside, and a good atmosphere is being created. It will take several matches for all of Coventry's willing singers to select a suitable site as their permanent stronghold, but for the present, a small enthusiastic choir have assembled in the near corner of the NTL West Stand. They cannot be faulted for effort, but the two thousand City followers are drowning them out vocally.

On the opposite side, the seats of the Marconi East Stand back onto an enormous conference centre, which houses 46 pitch-view rooms, 17 apartments, a hotel, a restaurant, and countless other rooms for conferences and banqueting. Consequently, a large white wall runs the length of the stand, provoking the illusion that we are indoors. In the middle of the wall are a number of smoked glass windows, which shield the corporate prawn sandwich brigade: smoked glass so that we can't see the backs of their heads. Either side of the windows are a couple of huge inviting white spaces, just crying out for a scoreboard and a fucking great big clock. I promise myself that I shall return to this ground one day – when it's finished.

Coventry enjoy a greater share of possession in the second half and regularly play the ball in to the feet of their strikers. Their passing is far more zippy: maybe the sprinklers had been turned on at the request of Micky Adams. City's passes meanwhile, are now failing to reach their target; it's almost as though the grass has grown a couple of inches since three o'clock.

On 72 minutes, Lynch makes a clumsy challenge on the edge of the box and receives his second yellow card. We are down to ten men and Coventry have a free kick in a dangerous position.

Thankfully, this is not the pivotal point of the game. That crucial moment is hijacked four minutes later by John Welch with a goal of pure class. He steals possession in midfield; beats three players and then pauses on the edge of the area, before curling the perfect chip into the top corner. The England Under 21 is mobbed by his team mates, and they all end up in a heap on the ground. Up in the Jewson Stand, we all mob each other and end up in heaps on the seats.

The goal kills off Coventry's comeback aspirations, and despite their numerical advantage, they are unable to muster a serious attack on goal. The fickle Sky Blue fans concede defeat and leave the 'Arena' in their droves. It is a wonderful sight to behold. Not since England's 5-1 victory in Munich have I enjoyed the sight of such an exodus. A friend of mine who attended that match regarded Steven Gerard's nutmeg on Deitmar Hamman as the high point, as it caused 10 000 Germans to rise in unison to escape further torture.

It is a welcome three points for the Tigers and they shoot up to mid-table respectability. The season is merely ten games old, so I find myself looking at the play-off places again, rather than the relegation zone. Emma is clearly a lucky mascot for City; maybe I should scrap the scheme of bringing a different guest to each match and stick with her.

Mind you, she has not been particularly attentive in the second half. She has spent most of it busily checking her mobile for the latest Premiership scores. Despite City's successful afternoon, she is not in the best of moods. Her beloved Everton have lost at home to Wigan. She had wrongly assumed that this home banker would herald the beginning of an Everton resurgence after a dodgy start to the season. Instead, it has only succeeded in placing David Moyes' head firmly on the chopping block.

She is not too happy about other results either. Before today, she was sitting at the top of a local fantasy football league (containing 37 other teams) but this afternoon's games have not been very productive. Her decision to replace Frank Lampard with John Terry as captain has backfired: Lampard has scored twice. That would have been double points, apparently. Other key players have been under-achieving too, and suddenly she goes all mathematical on me as she explains the points system and works out this week's tally. I pretend to be interested; it's the least I can do. She's just given up her Saturday afternoon to support a side that she knows little about. This fantasy stuff is OK, but I prefer the real deal, and today, City were just that.

COMPANION 6

Name: Michael McGeown
Birthplace: Johannesburg, South Africa
Relationship: Cousin
Allegiance: Hull City

Relevant History

Michael was only seven years old when we first went to a game together. His family had just relocated to Farnborough, which prompted his father (my Uncle Hughie) to relentlessly taunt us about Hull City's current inability to beat, even the likes of Aldershot. My Dad took offence to this and seized upon the chance to ram the insults down his throat: he drove the family down for a weekend in Hampshire to coincide with the early season Aldershot encounter.

Five of us took our seats in the 'best stand' of the piddly little Recreation Ground. My Dad, my brother Peter and I were all discreetly supporting the Tigers; Michael wasn't sure, but Uncle Hughie was siding with Aldershot, just so that he could maintain the jibes for another year. He had actually been a fervent City fan back in the 1960's and had partnered my Dad to many a battle at Boothferry Park, before heading off for a ten-year stint in South Africa. It saddened me that he had somehow lost his footballing way during those wilderness years, and was now making such a show of supporting his new local side.

Residents of the 'army town' were out in force and the tiny ground seemed quite full, although the attendance was actually only 2,345. The 'best stand' would undoubtedly rank as the 'worst stand' at most other grounds, and behind the goal to our left, there was no stand at all. A huge expanse of netting had been erected to prevent wayward shots from reaching the adjacent main road. At least Whitehurst and Flounders would be able to go home and claim that they had found the net a few times.

Fortunately, Gareth Roberts and Steve McLaren did find the net (the correct one), and it looked like game over when Billy Askew brilliantly chipped the stranded Shots keeper for a third, but a desperate defender chose to display his goalkeeping credentials by palming it over the bar. He was sent for an early bath and a penalty was awarded, but we missed it. Within no time, they had pegged it back to 2-1 and we were forced to endure a nervy last ten minutes. It seemed most unfair that Askew's genius had gone unrewarded. His exquisite chip should have been the icing on the cake in a convincing 3-0 demolition job, but instead, we had to hang on.

The excitement was too much for Peter and me, and we totally blew our cover. A few Aldershot fans were clearly not happy that we had infiltrated their ranks, and one or two missiles whistled dangerously past our ears. Well, I say missiles: they were actually screwed up sweet wrappers, but the intent was clear. At the final whistle we accordingly scaled down our celebrations.

It turned out to be a pivotal moment in our season. The victory helped us to climb into tenth position, and by January, we were top. We remained amongst the promotion places until May and eventually finished as runners-up. Uncle Hughie had been silenced, and young Michael had had a healthy dose of Hull City injected into his receptive little veins. Once the Tigers get into your system, there is no getting them out; I should know.

Unfortunately, though, he lived three hundred miles away from Hull, and this distance reduced the effectiveness of my indoctrination programme, so it was frustratingly impossible to build on Michael's early exposure to the Tigers. Naturally, he was strongly influenced by his friends and he lost the plot a bit during his teens. Then came those dangerous years away at University, where he followed the slippery slope of so many foolish students before him, by dabbling with Premiership clubs.

The time has come to set him back on his original path, and complete the job that I so competently started back in 1982.

VENUE 6 – CARROW ROAD

Norwich City 2 Hull City 1

Tuesday 27th September 2005 – 7.45pm

As everybody knows, a teacher's day ends at 3.30 on the dot and they are not required to think about school until 9 o'clock the following morning. Lessons are automatically prepared and books magically marked. The 7.45 Tuesday night kick off in Norwich, therefore, is only a minor inconvenience.

I join the M25 before the height of the rush hour, but the traffic is already beginning to build. It is a three-hour drive across uninspiring terrain, but I reach my destination by 7 o'clock to embark on the well nigh impossible task of finding a cheap parking space in an unfamiliar town, in fading light.

Michael has beaten me to Norwich by a good two hours. He took the 3 o'clock train out of London and has absorbed some culture by touring the cathedral and parts of the city centre. Meanwhile, I have wasted a further half an hour on a fruitless search for parking spaces. I wind up in a Morrison's Supermarket forecourt, just glad of a chance to get out and stretch my legs. I phone Michael: he has just been buying some grub (in Morrison's) and he is standing about twenty metres away from me. We make eye contact and he offers me a heated chicken and mushroom pie as a welcome gift, which I accept, although huge quantities of sweets are weighing heavy in my stomach from the long journey. I cautiously bite into the pie, not wanting to burn my tongue. Mmmm, interesting: the stone cold chunks of chicken on the inside provide an unexpected contrast to the piping-hot outer crust. Visions flash through my mind of a long and lonely night on the toilet; draining and straining; hurting and squirting, but manners overrule wisdom and I politely scoff the lot. Oh well, I could do with a day off school tomorrow.

I ask some canary coloured locals if the Morrison's parking facilities can be used by the football fans, but they point to a sign which stresses that waiting is restricted to thirty minutes. Blimey, the people of Norwich must do their weekly family shopping in a hurry! I've never managed to get under the hour myself. I settle for the nearby multi-story, where I am stung for £2.60: better than a ticket or a clamp.

The bright floodlights of Carrow Road are just across the dual-carriage way. Kick off time is near and the area around the ground is very busy. There are masses of Tigers fans in evidence, which is most commendable for an evening fixture in the middle the week, in the middle of nowhere. No sign of Delia yet though. As we make our way round to turnstiles 56 and 57, I realise that our tickets have placed us in Row Z. Looks like we'll be dodging Delaney's clearances for most of the night, and probably some of his passes as well.

Michael is glad that he plumped for the earlier train. He receives a text from his work colleague (a Norwich fan) who risked the later 5 o'clock option. It has been delayed and he still hasn't reached Norwich Station. City score in the first minute (a towering header from Leon Cort) and Michael immediately texts him back with the great news. He will surely think that it's a wind up.

The goal sets me off dreaming again. If we win here and then again at home to Millwall on Friday, we'll be up in the play off places, but Norwich are soon serving up a few doses of reality, and the fantasies fade. Darren Huckerby is causing havoc out on the left, and whenever any Norwich player receives the ball, they immediately spray it out to his touchline-hugging position. City appear content to allow him this freedom, rather than risk stretching the back four away from its pre-programmed shape. It surprises me that Huckerby has never been given a bash in the wide left role for England: every other left footed player in the country seems to have been auditioned; not to mention the right footers. Statistically, only one in nine people are left footed, so any leftie worth his salt should easily nail a place. Consider the list of recent applicants: Steve Guppy, Emile Heskey, Owen Hargreaves, Wayne Bridge, Trevor Sinclair, Joe Cole, and even, our own Nick Barmby. Surely, Huckerby would have fared no worse than any of these square pegs.

The equaliser comes on fifteen minutes, when a Norwich corner is sneakily passed outside the box to Youssef Safri (a good traditional Norfolk name there). Our sleepy defence allow him bags of time and space to tee up his shot, before launching it like a missile into the bottom corner of the net. Michael turns his mobile off, just in case.

The crowd now excitedly chant Youssef's name with his every touch, but they are unable to synchronise their Youssefs, and it just sounds like they are booing him. Fine, it saves us the trouble.

A few near misses later, Gary Doherty steals into the box, unmarked, to head them into the lead. I fear that the Tigers may be in for a bit of a mauling, so the half-time whistle brings welcome relief. We seek some refreshment at the bar and view the first half highlights on the TV screens. 'Who was picking up Doherty!!??'

Whilst dreamily glaring at the third re-run of the goals, I feel a tap on my shoulder: it's my Mum's neighbours from up in Hull, Dave and Sandie. I know them well as they are also the in-laws of my best mate (another Dave) but they are not normally renowned for their adventurous away treks in mid-week. They apparently were on their way to visit friends in West London but had made a detour for the sake of the Tigers. Obviously, the fact that Norwich is nearly a hundred miles off the beaten track has not deterred them. And I thought *I* was mad.

Back on the pitch, City re-start with a different formation. Chris Brown has been sacrificed (not on the altar unfortunately) and Stuart Green has been brought on to create a five-man midfield. Price fills in on the right, and Ryan France is clearly shitting his pants, because he has been told to mark Huckerby. The plan works – to a certain extent: the supply of passes to the left wing is cut off at source, but France keeps tight just in case. We enjoy more possession, but Craig Fagan is playing as a lone striker and is smothered by three Norwich defenders whenever he gets a sniff.

The singing from the City faithful is incessant and I put it to Michael that if we do manage to score, it will be entirely due to the lift that the travelling support has provided. A theory then begins to form in my mind as I think back over the previous away games. We only seem to be gaining points in matches where our support is behind the goal. The evidence speaks for itself:

Sheff. Wed.	Behind	Drew
Wolves	Side	Lost
Plymouth	Behind	Won
Palace	Side	Lost
Coventry	Behind	Won
Norwich	Side	Losing

It has long been my belief that the away fans should be tucked away in a corner at the KC Stadium, and made to feel inconsequential. The seats behind both goals should be jam-packed with City supporters to suck the ball into the net – or blow it out – as the case may be. There is no doubt in my mind that we have played our most enterprising football over the last three years, when attacking towards our own fans. One to consider there for the 'powers that be.'

Despite our tuneful encouragement, we are unable to worry the Norwich defence, and none of their back four find a use for Row Z. It is yet another narrow defeat. Sooner or later, we must turn these narrow defeats into draws, and the draws into narrow wins, otherwise we may be staring at a relegation dogfight.

Michael rushes off for his 10 o'clock train, and I am left to join the near stationary line of cars attempting to get away from Carrow Road. I'm going nowhere fast, so I phone Dave, back in Hull, to deliver a match report and to let him know that I saw the 'outlaws.' He finds it most amusing that I should be stuck in the middle of Norwich at such a late hour with no prospect of sleep until the early hours of Wednesday. As if his scorn is not enough, he then deals me another cruel blow with the information that he is about to go to bed. The futility of the whole exercise now strikes me, and I hit a real low point. I could have relaxed with a beer this evening, and watched Champions League football in the comfort of my own home; but instead, I'm here, in deepest Norfolk, with matchsticks between my eyelids, bracing myself for the dark and lonely drive home, after a tame 2-1 defeat.

The journey back is indeed long and exhausting, but I fend off dreamland by chain-chewing a succession of Jelly Babies and Chocolate Éclairs. By one o'clock in the morning, though, I am in serious need of a bucket. The sickly concoction of jelly and toffee has met up with the pre-match salmonella pie, and the omens are not good.

I finally crawl into my welcoming bed at 1.30am, but typically, I am now wide-awake. My gurgling stomach is still trying to make sense of today's mixed offerings, but I gradually drift off to sleep, well aware that my clock-radio alarm will cheerily burst into life in just four and a half hours time. That will be the next low point.

COMPANION 7

Name: Malcolm Hill
Birthplace: Aylesbury
Relationship: College friend
Allegiance: Luton Town

Relevant History

I have made four visits to Kenilworth Road – all with Malcolm. The first two trips were in the 1980's, when Luton had cheated their way into the First Division by installing a plastic pitch that nobody else could handle. The Hatters had developed a neat one-touch passing game, more akin to five-a-sides, and as a consequence, their impressive home form ensured top-flight tenure for a number of seasons.

Manchester United were the opponents on my first visit. I remember very little from the game, except that United employed Bryan Robson as a sweeper to snuff out the threat of Paul Walsh and Mark Stein. It must have worked as it resulted in a 0-0 stalemate.

Next up were Everton, and this game is notable for a little bet that we placed beforehand to predict the first goalscorer. Malcolm played safe, and went for a 7-1 Mick Harford, while I could not resist a flutter on Everton's generously priced 33-1 marauding left back, Neil Pointon. He had notched a few goals recently with his overlapping forward raids, and seemed like a good outside bet. The odds didn't appear quite so generous when we reached the terraces and took in the team news. Pointon wasn't playing. He wasn't even sub. He was injured. He probably wasn't even in Luton. No wonder the girl behind the counter had been so keen to snatch my money.

Malcolm and I have been good friends since 1981, but it took until the 2001-02 season for Luton and Hull to meet in the league. We went together and sat amongst the Luton fans: not a pleasant experience. I longed to be with the Tigers contingent, especially when Greg Matthews put us ahead, early in the second half. We found it surprisingly easy to hold out for the 1-0 win on that night, which lifted us into second place and left an ineffective Luton side in fifth.

It was most satisfying to eves-drop on the pessimistic Hatter chatter as we filed out of the ground. The general consensus seemed to be that Luton were heading nowhere, and Hull were looking like a good bet for promotion. Who would have thought that by the end of the season, Luton would be pipped for the championship in a two horse race with Plymouth, 36 points ahead of City.

But then again, who would have dreamt, that by February 2005, Malcolm and I would be returning to watch the same two sides battle it out at the top of League One. Again, we occupied the Luton end and we were joined by his 16 year-old son, Christopher. Despite living in Twickenham, poor Christopher has been systematically brainwashed since birth, so he now worships Luton too.

Stuart Elliott had been scoring goals for fun before Christmas, but he was still out with a fractured cheekbone. His replacement for this game appeared to be Junior Lewis, but for large parts of the game, nobody seemed to be covering the left side at all. Lewis had taken a bit of stick from the fans in previous weeks, but Peter Taylor had stuck by him, claiming that he did the simple things well; like tying up his bootlaces presumably, or pulling on his shirt, or running out onto the pitch. Certainly, when the match got under way, the complicated instruction to stay out on the left appeared to be beyond him.

The great Johan Cruyff once tried to explain the secret of his own brilliance by declaring, "I have an instinct to do the wrong things." Junior was clearly gifted with the same instinct – he just had different results.

Lewis was joined in midfield by the diminutive figure of new signing, Andy Hessenthaler. The transfer policy at this stage of the season was to bolster the squad with players of limited quality, who were cheap and did the job – very much like 'value' products from Tesco's. Luton's midfield soon realised that if they kept the ball higher than 5' 6" in the air,

Hessenthaler couldn't get near it. It was a bit like watching a yappy little terrier chasing after a Frisbee on a beach, thrown by children who were skilful enough and cruel enough to keep it just out of the dog's reach.

In fact, Hess was in for a pretty miserable afternoon all round. The worst crime that you can commit in the Bedfordshire region is to be an ex-Watford player. Even though his Watford days had been early in his career (about thirty years ago in Hessenthaler's case) the crowd still rose as one whenever the ball went near him, to hurl a torrent of vitriolic abuse in his direction. Consequently, our midfield was completely overrun, and only a combination of wasteful Luton finishing and excellent goalkeeping from Myhill kept it level.

We fared much better in the second half. The pacy Facey replaced the wooden Wilbraham, and as full time approached, it was the Tigers who were looking the more likely. But, in the 89th minute, Luton launched a final unchallenged raid down their vacant right wing, and whipped in a cross for Brkovic to head the winner. The Sunday papers described him as the smallest man on the pitch, although Hessenthaler might have had something to say about that. Malcolm, Christopher and all of the Luton fans went mental of course, and I was trapped right in the middle of them.

My initial reaction was to sit with my head in my hands, but an innate survival instinct promptly kicked in, forcing me to stand and applaud politely in an attempt to look a little less conspicuous. In hindsight, it may have been a blessing that City did not steal the late winner; I would almost certainly have leapt up in celebration, inviting the mad Hatters around me to vent some of their Hessenthaler hatred.

I'm unable to recall a moment in football where I have been more eager for the ground to open wide and swallow me up. Malcolm and Christopher were really in my face with their over the top gloating, and a long friendship was in serious danger of coming to an abrupt end. The whole stand had found its voice again and was singing at maximum volume about winning the league. I couldn't get away from the place fast enough and the phrase 'beam me up Scottie' had never seemed more relevant.

Still, I did suddenly feel more cheerful when we got back to Malcolm's car. It had been clamped, and he had to pay £85 to get free. That wiped the fucking smile off his face.

VENUE 7 – ST. MARY'S STADIUM

Southampton 1 Hull City 1

Saturday 15th October 2005 – 3pm

The Dell had been Southampton's home for 103 years, so it was well past its sell-by date. However: its age, its limited capacity, and the crowd's close proximity to the pitch, all combined to make it an awkward little ground to take points from. It became something of a fortress and was largely responsible for the Saints twenty-seven year stay in the top flight.

It was hardly surprising, that in 2001, the city had mixed feelings about relocating to a new 32 000 all-seater stadium on the banks of the River Itchen. The pessimists were initially vindicated when the 2001 season began poorly, and stories abounded that the stadium was cursed, having been built on top of an old graveyard. An exorcist was called in, and his visit spookily coincided with an upturn in fortunes, but sadly, his work came with only a standard four-year guarantee, and in 2005 they were finally relegated.

The harsh reality is, that the ownership of a magnificent new home generates one major drawback; everyone looks forward to visiting. This is definitely the case for me; it was one of the first fixtures that I looked for when the list was announced, and today's unusually warm mid-October sunshine (21°C) should help to make it the perfect day out. I already know that City cannot lose because we are sitting in the Northam Stand, behind the goal, and my new theory dictates that we only lose when we sit at the side.

Malcolm drives us straight into the heart of Southampton, and the signposts soon bring us directly to the sparkling new glass-fronted 'Friends Provident St. Mary's Stadium.' We are supposed to be meeting my brother, Peter, in a pub called the Dolphin, so we ask a policeman for directions, but these are far too complicated and we stop listening after the third step. A hundred yards further on, there is a handy car park for £5 with a pub right next door, so sod it; I phone Peter and arrange to meet him later at the ground.

We pop into the Coopers Arms, and once again, I come face to face with the father-in-law of Dave, my best mate from Hull (he also appeared at the Norwich game, remember?) I'm starting to get suspicious; I hope he's not writing a book. We join him for a couple of beers before strolling out into the unseasonal heat wave: this global warming thing; I'm all for it!

Outside the stadium, Malcolm links up with Andy, a Southampton-based work colleague. He has a haunted look about him and I soon discover why. A month ago, he had taken his football crazy son to the Luton v Southampton game as part of a corporate hospitality package. Luton had no mascot for the day, so his son was asked if he would like to fill the void. Andy reluctantly agreed, judging that it would be a great experience and that it couldn't do him any harm. How wrong he was. The boy enjoyed the day so much that he is now a Luton convert. Malcolm immediately gets to work with further words of encouragement and indoctrination.

Over by the programme vendor I spy my brother, with his friend, Suff. Peter seems relieved to have a ticket in his hand. Last night on the phone, he had optimistically explained to me that he was going to collect it in an unnamed pub, somewhere in Southampton, from someone he didn't know. It was all arranged through the Southern Supporters Club, but it sounded a bit risky to me.

Time is short, so we agree to meet up again at half time by the bar. Malcolm and I make it to our places, which are over to one side of the goal. The prime seats, in the centre, right behind the goal, are all wastefully empty and are being used as a buffer zone between the two sets of supporters. It is undeniably a very well designed and tidy stadium, almost too tidy. It makes me question whether many of these new stadiums will end up looking the same. Will they be so perfectly constructed as to have no character? At St. Mary's, seats rise up to the same level on all sides and there are no tiers, so none of the stands possess any distinguishing features. If it wasn't for the scoreboard at the far end, players could easily lose their bearings and forget which way they were kicking; the first half is so uneventful that I begin to wonder.

Alternative entertainment is provided by an ongoing situation at the top of the stand, involving some over-officious stewards. They are getting quite stroppy with some of our more boisterous followers, and are threatening to remove them from the ground if they refuse to sit down. A small piece in the programme explains:

"People who stand are in breach of ground regulation 9, and persistent standing may result in an ejection." Malcolm tries standing a few times but then gives up, realising that he has mis-read the programme. He thought it said, "…may result in an erection."

Now, one might argue that the poor stewards were just trying to do their job, but a few rows away, about two thousand Southampton fans are blatantly remaining on their feet throughout the whole commotion, and no one makes the slightest attempt to sit them down.

Half time is near, and Malcolm gallantly offers to join the queue at the bar. Before he can leave his seat however, Matthew Oakley unleashes an unstoppable 25-yard effort through a crowded penalty area into the roof of the net: Myhill doesn't see it. City are stung into life by this, and they nearly equalise, twice, before the break. First, Fagan comes close, and then France has a header tipped over by Antti Niemi. More has happened in this three-minute spell than in the rest of the first half.

When we finally find Peter and Suff during the break, they are not in a relaxed state. They have been sitting right in the middle of the rebellious element, and are finding themselves 'between a rock and a hard place.' In order to see the action, they are forced to stand, but the stewards are threatening to haul them out if they don't sit. It's a 'no win' situation, and I feel that an ejection would be most unfair. There again, I've probably been guilty of similar injustices in the classroom: "Right, that's it! I don't care who it was; you're all staying in at break-time!"

When Malcolm and I return to our seats, we scan the crowd to locate my brother's position. He really is in the thick of it, but at least he is in the shade. The intense afternoon sun has now dropped, and the roof of our stand no longer provides protection. Many arms are raised to shield squinting eyes: there will be a few aching limbs in 45 minutes time.

The Saints raise their game, and some solid defending is required to keep it at 1-0, but with twenty minutes remaining, Peter Taylor decides that it is time for a masterstroke of a substitution. On come Burgess and Ellison. Big Ben immediately sets about winning every available header, and suddenly we're looking more dangerous. Fagan comes back to life, and he fights to win possession from a long Myhill clearance. He flicks it through for Ellison, and the shaven-headed winger drives purposefully into the box like a man possessed, before walloping an unstoppable strike past the shell-shocked Niemi.

This well-deserved equaliser brings the alarmingly twitchy Harry Redknapp to the edge of the technical area. His jerks and gestures are heading into overdrive, and I fear that if city score a winner, he may have to be carted off in a straight-jacket. This will be Southampton's eighth consecutive draw, and he is desperately in need of a win to keep in touch with the play-off contenders. He definitely won't be relishing the prospect of a little visit from Sir Clive Woodward after the game to let him know exactly where he's going wrong. The mastermind of the disastrous Lions tour 'Down Under' has been given his own column in the programme, to keep fans informed of his role within the club. Nobody will be any the wiser after reading it.

The first two months have been primarily observational, although I'm sure he's already picking up a fat-cat salary. Having settled in, he stresses that he's now ready to 'get his hands dirty.' Hmm, a little stint helping the groundsmen maybe. Apparently, the next phase of his master plan, is to study each player, one by one, looking at all aspects of their performance, with the aim of making them better players. The guy is a sodding genius. I'm sure Harry would never have thought of doing that. Unfortunately, he stops short of telling us how he will actually achieve this. He must be saving that for next week's programme.

The St. Mary's seats are rapidly emptying; everyone can see the inevitable draw coming, and they all go for the quick getaway, followed possibly by a spot of sunbathing on the beach before sundown. The Tigers fans, though, are in party mode, and we're all on our feet, merrily flouting ground regulation 9. Malcolm goes with the flow and he's having a good time until a text comes through which tells of Luton's 3-1 defeat at bottom club, Crewe. Even worse, his daughter, Sarah, has been at Stamford Bridge with friends for her first football match, and has witnessed a thrilling second half comeback by the Blues which helps them to sweep away a stubborn Bolton, by five goals to one. She sends a text to inform him that she now supports Chelsea.

Later on, as we enjoy a fish and chip supper in Malcolm's kitchen, his seventeen-year old son, Christopher seems a little concerned. His sister is chomping her chips, clad totally in Chelsea gear, and his father is talking enthusiastically about Ellison's late equaliser. The house is no longer a Luton stronghold. Maybe I will enlist Christopher as a future guest and completely wipe out the Hatters virus. Is he too old to be the Tigers mascot I wonder?

COMPANION 8

Name: Ben Cawthorn
Birthplace: Lytham St. Annes
Relationship: College friend
Allegiance: Bolton Wanderers

Relevant History

In my first year at college, I lived on the same corridor as Ben, but the only communication that existed between us was a series of polite nods as we passed on the stairs. After all, he had long curly hair and always sported a fluffy, green, baggy jumper. Mum had warned me about these junky hippie wasters. Then, during a Geography field trip to Norfolk, we shared a beer or two and I realised that he was nothing more than a harmless laid-back northerner with a similar juvenile sense of humour to my own. He was a Blackpool follower, but was mad on Manchester United although he has recently 'come out' as a Bolton fan.

By the third year, Ben and I were sharing the same run-down house along with three other Geographers: Malcolm, Bill and Richard. Malcolm was crazy about Luton Town, whereas Bill came from Wales, so couldn't see past rugby. The fifth member of the household, Richard, held a passing interest in football, but was not fanatical; a fact that I was easily able to deduce within seconds of our introduction. He hailed from Bristol so the obvious opening enquiry just had to be:

"Rovers or City?"

The reply was a disappointment.

"Well, I suppose if I had to choose..."

That said it all. He should have bloody chosen about fifteen years ago and then stuck solidly to that choice through thick and thin. There were no further questions.

I'll give him his due though. He often strived manfully (but foolishly) to join in our heated football debates. Big mistake. I mean, I would never try to engage Tony Blair in a conversation about Labour Party policies: it would soon become patently obvious that I possessed less than one percent of the knowledge required to maintain a sensible discussion. But Richard would regularly swim into deep and dangerous waters, such as the merits of the 4-4-2 system, or the Dutch deployment of 'total football' at the 1974 World Cup. At such junctures, he would always drown horribly before drifting quietly away to try his luck with Bill and rugby.

As a woefully inadequate substitute for Blackpool, Luton and Hull, the three of us adopted Brentford as our new, but temporary obsession. After a few enjoyable days out at Griffin Park, we had found ourselves some new heroes. Francis Joseph was smashing the goals in up front, while in midfield, Terry Hurlock was smashing in a few shins. We were even treated to one or two cameo appearances from Stan Bowles in the twilight of his career.

Occasionally, we would invite along a guest to check out our new local side. One week we made a dreadful mistake by trying to educate an American friend in the ways of 'real' football. Evan was on a one-year exchange from Santa Clara University in California and was an extremely nice bloke – but – like most Americans, he didn't know how to keep his voice down in public. Each time that he made a bellowing observation about the Brentford dee-fence, Ben and I would edge a little further along the terrace, leaving Malcolm to field all the embarrassing questions. As Evan got more involved in the action, so the volume shot up. He became particularly excited whenever Keith Cassells received the ball. Cassells had earned himself the nickname of 'Chicken George', thanks to an uncanny resemblance to the character from Roots, a BBC dramatisation of the slave trade.

"Yey! Go Chicken George, go!" he would yell at regular intervals, with no apparent concern for the attention that he was attracting. The crowd around us soon recognised our plight and gained great entertainment from the little sideshow. They quickly got to know our names.

Evan's real 'piece de resistance' came during the second half when he noticed that Cassells was a bit bow-legged. It was common knowledge within our household that *my* legs did not exactly follow the shortest route to the ground either, but this information, so far, had not become part of the public domain – until – without warning, in the quietest part of the match, Evan suddenly bleated out:

"HEY, HE'S GOT BANDY LEGS LIKE YOU PAUL!!"

With utter resignation, I bowed my head, closed my eyes and buried my face in my hands, as hundreds of fans in the immediate vicinity craned their necks to get a good look at my legs. No way was he coming to the next game. The next game was the big one. The Tigers were in town.

I still had to find a guest for the crunch match as Ben and Malcolm had made it crystal clear that they would be occupying the Brentford end. I couldn't possibly risk taking Evan in amongst the City die-hards. He would surely drop me in it as a part time Bees supporter and get both of our heads thoroughly kicked in. Instead, I persuaded Simon: a Manchester City and Bournemouth fan. Yes, a strange mix, but he was born in Manchester and moved to Bournemouth when he was thirteen so had a legitimate right to follow both.

It was a typical English October day: grotty, wet, wild and windy; not at all conducive to a flowing game of football, but our spirits were not dampened as we took up our rival positions on the terraces. Simon and I joined the City faithful on the far side from the dugouts. We could easily pick out the distinctive figures of Ben and Malcolm down at pitch level almost directly opposite us, in an area known as the 'Paddock' – very similar to the 'Well' at Boothferry Park. It was all set up.

The Brentford side had managed to worm its way into my affections over the previous months, but today I hated them. They were very much the enemy as they worked to halt City's march up the league tables. My loathing of Francis Joseph intensified when he put Brentford ahead in the first half. The opposite feelings were in evidence across the pitch where Joseph's cult hero status was confirmed, and Ben and Malcolm performed an exaggerated celebratory jig. The annoying pair made absolutely sure that Simon and I were aware of their joy by continuing the merry little dance for a full five minutes after the goal.

City improved in the second half, but the outcome was still looking as bleak as the weather. Then, in the last minute, Les Mutrie popped up with an equaliser, prompting Simon and I to mimic the goal-dance all the way through to the final whistle.

In the distance, I could just make out two sad, dripping, motionless statues. Their plans for a protracted evening of piss-taking lay in ruins. I will never be able to thank Les Mutrie enough.

VENUE 8 – TURF MOOR

Burnley 1 Hull City 0
Friday 28th October 2005 – 7.45pm

Now, pay attention! These next few days are extremely complicated. Here is the proposed timetable:

- Friday: whole family drive to Preston (in two cars) for a two-night hotel stopover
- I detour to Ben's house in Warrington while the family head for a hotel in Preston
- Ben drives me to the Burnley match and then drops me back at the Preston hotel
- My car stays outside Ben's house in Warrington
- Saturday: happy family day out in the Lake District
- Sunday: all return south in Patsy's car
- Tuesday: tear out of school and get a train for Preston
- Gary picks me up and takes me to Preston v City
- Gary drops me in Warrington after the game on the way back to his Liverpool home
- Crash out at Ben's house
- Wednesday, 5am: reunited with my car to drive back to Hemel Hempstead
- 8.30am – arrive at school for a full day's teaching.

"Foolproof," Ben cries, when I explain the plan to him over the phone. Fortunately, I am not superstitious, or I would have been worried by his splendid example of fate tempting.

However, the hand of fate is resting on my shoulder as early as 11am on the Friday when we hit the tailback from an accident at Toddington Services. The M6 is not much better, and it's stop/start all the way to Cheshire. My radio belatedly warns me that today is one of the worst days of the year for traffic congestion – this is not really much help.

I reach Ben's by mid-afternoon, and already, matters have been complicated by a slight change of plan. I have arrived with an extra passenger, my 6 year-old son, Stephen. He had suddenly decided at Stafford Services that he definitely wanted to come to the game, so he swapped cars. This is fine; it's not an all ticket match so I can pay for him on the gate. It will be his first football match, so privately, I'm pleased and proud, although it does heap extra pressure on the Tigers to pull off a spectacular victory in order to secure his undying support for the next 70 years or so. He is a fickle chap by nature, and thanks to some influential school friends, his present leaning is towards Watford. A heavy defeat tonight could even swing him Burnley's way.

Worried about the possibility of Friday night gridlock in the Lancastrian conurbations, the three of us set off extra early. As we make our way out onto the M6 and across to the M65, I realise that the region is densely populated with Premiership clubs. En route, we pass signs for Wigan, Bolton and Blackburn, while Manchester and Liverpool are not far behind us; that's seven clubs within a fifteen-mile radius. Looks like I'll be making quite a few trips up to this neck of the woods next season when we hit the big time!

Even though we are somewhat early, parking is surprisingly easy. We pass the time by visiting the club shop and circumnavigating the ground, although we discover that this is not possible, and have to turn back after nosing around outside the Sky TV van. The presence of the cameras could well explain why the crowds are still very thin on the ground. Many locals have obviously elected to spend their Friday night by the telly, or down the boozer.

We take our seats in good time, and I have to admit that it's a half decent ground, which by definition, means that the other half must be crap. The Tigers fans, of course, have been placed in the crap half. The seats are ancient wooden ones and they make a deafening whack whenever they are lowered or raised. Should this cause annoyance; one has the option of moving to quieter seats, where the heavy wooden flaps have long-since been removed; offering the alternative attraction of becoming impaled on the remaining metal prongs. These decrepit facilities are in stark contrast to the James Hargreaves Stand to our left, and the Jimmy McIlroy Stand, directly opposite. Both of these are relatively new two-tiered structures that would grace any Premiership ground. If the other half of the ground mirrored these, it would indeed be a fine stadium.

The action begins, and the City fans are in excellent voice: so is Stephen, but he hasn't yet grasped that we are watching Burnley against Hull City, and he insists on cheering for Watford. A number of aggressive youths behind us seem unconcerned by his neutral status; in fact, they seem completely unaware that a six year old is within ear-shot, and we are treated to their full repertoire of swear words as they bawl vehement abuse towards the pitch.

Swearing apart, Ben is staggered by the incredible noise that the Tigers end generates. All the old favourites are being churned out, and we happily sing along, although we are not quite sure of the lyrical relevance of one number, where we rejoice the fact that there is only one Tony Blackburn. As far as I am aware, the aging DJ has no connection with this fixture, so we listen more closely, and the penny drops. "Small town near Blackburn..." is the lyric, "...you're just a small town near Blackburn..."

The Tigers are on top. An air-born Chris Brown directs a diving header at goal, only for Brian Jensen to perform a spectacular diving save (that's two players who haven't forgotten that the TV cameras are here). Ryan France misses a great chance at the far post, but Ade Akinbiyi then decides to invoke 'Sod's Law'. Under Peter Taylor at Leicester, he had been unable to hit a barn door; so tonight, typically, he decides to play like a Brazilian. With ten minutes to go to half time, he gathers the ball in the box; juggles it; swivels, and hits a low shot across Myhill into the bottom corner of the net.

Moments later, he bursts through again, but he's now feeling a bit more like his old self and he skies the ball high into our stand, breaking a few more of the old wooden seats in the process.

We get to half time, and Stephen wants to go home. Ben probably does too, but he conceals his feelings as we sup a beer, and Stephen munches through his third chocolate bar of the night. Ben is in reflective mood, and he casts his mind back to his last Turf Moor visit. Manchester United provided the opposition on that day, and the crowds came flocking in from all over Lancashire, just to catch a glimpse of George Best. How ironic, that this evening, he should still be making the headlines as he clings to life in a hospital bed.

My only sighting of Bestie was at Boothferry Park in 1972, not for Manchester United, but for Northern Ireland, against Spain. Because of the sectarian troubles, the Irish games were played at a variety of English venues. City's player-manager, Terry Neill, was Northern Ireland's captain, but the 20 000 crowd were lured in purely by the prospect of witnessing the brilliance of Best. Unfortunately, the great man had a quiet game, and everyone soon realised that this was a match that they didn't actually want to see.

A similar feeling may well overcome me in tonight's game if matters don't soon improve. A host of chances are created at both ends in the second half, and Stuart Elliott is unlucky not to bag a hat-trick. He strikes the bar with a volley; has a header blocked on the line, and misses the post by inches with a deft lob.

The clock is ticking down, but then I remember my new theory: we are behind the goal, so we can't lose. It is announced over the public address system that Brian Jensen has been made Sky TV's Man of the Match. I can only remember him making two saves of note. The 'Hollywood' save in the first half from Brown clearly swung it for him.

Three minutes into stoppage time, the ball lands at the feet of Elliott, 15 yards out. He strikes it well, but Jensen is keen to underline his Man of the Match performance with one more leaping save whilst smiling at the cameras.

Time is up, and my 'behind the goal' theory has been overruled by the 'Sky Sports' theory, which decrees that we will lose 1-0 whenever their cameras are present. Burnley fans breath a sigh of relief, as they have been under the cosh towards the end. My son is also relieved, as he is bored, cold, tired and he wants more chocolate. Within minutes of getting back to Ben's car, he is fast asleep.

It is a short drive back along the M65 to Preston, and I am soon re-united with the rest of my family. Apart from the disappointing result, part one of my plan has been successfully completed. Part two might not be so straightforward.

COMPANION 9

Name: Gary Hogben
Birthplace: Hull
Relationship: School Friend
Allegiance: Hull City

Relevant History:

Gary and I were in the same class throughout secondary school and we always sat together in R.E. and French. A priest, commonly known as Pinhead, taught these lessons. He had acquired this nickname many years before, on account of his pointy balding summit, but he was a nice bloke and a good teacher, so Gary and I made good progress in his lessons.

Just occasionally, however, Pinhead was liable to flip; his face and head would go puce and he would utter naughty words – words not normally associated with a man of the cloth. During one French lesson, we were forced to 'excuse his French' as he strived in vain to focus our wayward attention on a map of Paris. Suddenly, the red mist descended, and he cried out, "Will you just look at the bastard map!"

The room fell silent. Had we heard him correctly? Had he just called the map a bastard? Surely, it wasn't the map's fault. *We* were the ones he should be calling bastards. He quickly regained his composure, and seemed very embarrassed by his outburst, but he had no need to be; it had done his street-cred the world of good.

A few weeks later, I thought that Gary was going to tip him over the edge again, when out of the blue he asked:

"Er...Father, what is the French for Pinhead?"

We braced ourselves for the backlash, but the response was surprisingly controlled.

"Ah well, you see Hogben," he began, "the French would not call it pin head; they would call it 'head of the pin' so it would be 'tête de l'épingle'. It's rather like seaside, where they would say, 'side of the sea' – bord de la mer, and..."

He went on to provide us with several more mind-numbing examples, which followed the same grammatical rule. Gary regretted his enquiry. It dawned on us that Pinhead may not actually be aware of his own nickname, even though it had been passed on through a complete generation of school children. Either that, or he had been attending anger management courses and had learnt to respond to flippant questions with long, drawn-out explanations that bored us into submission.

Some time later (in January 1981 to be precise) Gary pushed his luck with another daring question. Hull City had been drawn away to Tottenham in the fourth round of the F.A. Cup, so Gary put forward the fanciful proposal that Pinhead should drive a group of us down to London in the school mini-bus. Incredibly, he agreed. Even to this day, we are not sure why. Maybe it had been offered as a penance at his last confession.

Twenty-five years ago, school mini-buses were devoid of safety features. The seating consisted of two long wooden benches that ran the full length of the bus, so we all had to sit facing in towards the middle. There were no seat belts, of course, so whenever Pinhead applied the brakes, we all slid forwards and crushed the poor sods that had elected to sit near the front. Likewise, whenever he hit the accelerator too hard, we all shot to the back, and anyone seated by the rear doors would pray that the locking mechanism was secure enough to prevent an exit onto the fast lane of the M1. It was not the most comfortable of journeys.

But, we got there safely and managed to squeeze the bus into a parking space some way from Whitehart Lane. I had never been to a first division ground before, and on the approach to the stadium I was completely awe-struck by its sheer size. The ten minutes prior to kick-off were spent staring in wonder at the old 'shelf', high up in the misty sky, with a golden ball and cockerel perched on top. It looked almost surreal.

The tie got under way and the first thing that I noted was how Steve

Archibald played with his shirt hanging out. The fashion in 1981 was for ridiculously short shorts, so his lengthy flapping shirt kept us guessing as to whether he had remembered to don any shorts at all. Being a Scotsman, maybe he was used to wearing a kilt and he enjoyed the extra freedom that it offered to his genitals.

The early pace and movement of the Spurs men was very impressive. Glenn Hoddle was pulling the strings from midfield and I feared for the Tigers central defensive pairing of Steve Richards and Stuart Croft. Tony Norman, though, was in inspired form and was singularly responsible for keeping the game goalless until deep into the second half.

With ten minutes remaining, as a final throw of the dice, Spurs sent on Gary Brookes.

"Never heard of him," said Gary. "They're obviously getting desperate."

Two minutes later, Brookes hit a twenty-yard drive into the bottom corner of the net. Then they scored again. We would probably have settled for 2-0 before the game, but having come within eight minutes of a replay, we were gutted.

As Gary and I trudged towards the exit, we realised that we had become separated from our group and neither of us had the slightest clue where the bus was parked. Then, just as a mild panic was beginning to set in, we spotted it – 'la tête de l'épingle' was clearly visible in the distance, rising up above the heaving crowds. The glare from the floodlights reflected off his smooth dome, creating a shining beacon to safely guide us home.

The drive back was horrendous. It was dark and the traffic was bad. It took an age just to get out of London. As we eventually joined the M1, it became obvious that the sixteen boisterous teenagers in the back of the bus were going to severely test the driver's suspect temperament. There were at least four hours of boredom ahead, and with no seat belts to restrain us; we were jumping about like a cage full of chimps at feeding time.

I could see the back of Pinhead's neck beginning to glow red. He was a ticking time bomb. He finally exploded just past Nottingham, and swerved across to pull up on the hard shoulder. Some of the younger passengers (who had not so far ignored his classroom map of Paris) were in for a nasty shock. The second half of the journey was a lot quieter.

VENUE 9 – DEEPDALE

Preston North End 3 Hull City 0

Tuesday 1st November 2005 – 7.45pm

Ah yes…November 1st…Patsy's birthday! This was always going to be the awkward one. It's probably safe to say, that I am not the most popular husband in Hertfordshire today, although my wonderful wife has displayed remarkable patience and understanding. Actually, 'understanding' is not quite the right word; she doesn't understand me at all: she thinks that I have gone barking mad, and she may just be right.

I make it to Hemel Hempstead Station for 4pm. Two changes are needed; at Watford Junction and at Crewe, enabling me to arrive in Preston at 7.20pm. I am convinced that it's all going to go pear-shaped. I have foolishly placed all of my faith in the British railway network, building in only a 25-minute margin of error.

Incredibly though, each train arrives and departs at the exact given times, and I meet Gary at precisely 7.19pm, as planned. He has already booked a taxi and we make it to Deepdale with time to spare, but not enough time to check out the National Football Museum underneath the Sir Tom Finney Stand. Having travelled so far, it is disappointing to be missing this spectacle, and I could have picked up a souvenir birthday present for Patsy as well. She'll have to settle for a programme.

Loitering outside the museum is Damian, our old school friend. He has toured around it and he strongly recommends a visit, but we'll have to save it for next year, assuming Preston are still in the same division as us. The three of us collect our tickets and head inside.

On first inspection, Deepdale appears to have been expertly modified in readiness for the rigors of the 21st century, but closer examination reveals that the upgrade is embarrassingly incomplete. Last week, I classified Burnley's ground as being half decent. Deepdale is three-quarters decent, but the crap quarter far exceeds the crapiness of Burnley's crappy half.

The inferior stand consists chiefly of empty, crumbling, condemned terracing, but it also houses a small covered seating area, which is curiously off-centre. Symmetry was not a priority for the designer of this one. Apparently, the locals have dubbed this run-down mess, 'The ITV Digital Stand,' on account of the bankrupt company, which pulled the plug on the small fortune set aside for its reconstruction. Shame: the rest of the place looks good.

I'm beginning to take an interest in the distinctive design features of each stadium, and here, it is the elaborate floodlights that catch my eye. They are surrounded by a mass of white girders, which mesh together, forming buttresses to support the four main pylons: a sort of...posh scaffolding!

Down on the pitch, City's reorganised defence has lost its Edge, and its Dawson, and its Coles. Delaney fills the left back void, Marc Joseph tries his luck at centre half, and we struggle from the word go. Preston hit the post, Delaney makes a superb goal line stop, and Myhill is generally overworked. We ride our luck and reach half time, goalless, without having created any heart-stopping moments to worry the home crowd.

During the break, I produce from my pocket, an old letter that Gary had sent me, back in 1981. He had just started a course at Sunderland Polytechnic, so his first assignment was to attend the Tigers match at Hartlepool and file a report. We lost the encounter 3-2 and Gary was scathing in his write-up about the performance of our worst player ever, Stuart Eccleston. Somehow, Stoke had offloaded Eccleston to us with all the skill of a second hand car salesman, who is well aware of all the serious faults, but still convinces you that you have bought a good little runner. Well, Eccleston was not a good little runner; in fact he ran like a girl, and after two minutes of the Hartlepool encounter, he had conceded a penalty. The letter sparks off a quest to remember the worst City players in our living memory. Iain Hesford is unchallenged as the goalkeeper for our Nightmare XI, and so is the manager (Mark Hately), but midfield contenders are hard to come by. It seems that incompetence is less forgivable at the opposite ends of the pitch, and we are spoilt for choice with strikers and defenders.

Damian immediately throws Dave Sunley's name into the hat; just beating me to it. Nick Deacy, another player from the 1981 side, is also selected. We then recall that Deacy was signed by Mike Smith (the ex-Welsh national manager) so Smith is instantly appointed as Hately's assistant. Gavin Gordon is considered as a third striker, but escapes inclusion due to an inexplicably successful post-City spell with Lincoln.

In defence, Neil Buckley takes his place alongside Eccleston, but we have no time to discuss the full backs, as we need to return to our seats for the second half.

We begin well, and hopes are high that the match will perfectly fit the classic cliché, and become a 'game of two halves.' On 59 minutes, though, our defence is caught square, and the lively Jemal Johnson springs the offside trap to race clear and finish in style; belting the ball into the roof of the net.

Briefly, the Tigers rally, but two long-range efforts extinguish our hopes. David Jones fires in off the post and Paul McKenna finds the top corner from all of 30 yards. Suddenly, I feel like I'm a long way from home (which I am) and the final whistle cannot come quickly enough. It is our worst away performance of the season, and Preston's first home win. It seems that some of the City players on show tonight have been making a late bid to get into our Nightmare XI.

The chap who announces the results over the P.A. system then displays a cruel sense of humour. He runs through the Championship scores, and delivers with great relish, 'Preston 3 Hull City 0,' as if we need reminding.

After a couple of drinks, to drown our sorrows, Damian drops us back at the station, where Gary picks up his car to drive me to Warrington. To pass the time on the hour-long journey, we resurrect our search for clueless past players. A few more strikers come to mind: Alf Wood, Darren France, and how could we forget…Billy Woof! I think his name actually *was* spelt with an exclamation mark.

It is after midnight when Gary drops me at the end of Ben's street, and inevitably, as we are close to Manchester, it is lashing down with rain. I quickly sprint through the puddles, past my car, and into Ben's doorway, where I gently tap on the door so as not to wake his children. No answer. I knock a bit harder. Still no answer. I'm getting soaked, so sod the kids: I rap as hard as possible and ring the doorbell. Little seeds of panic begin to grow in my mind, as once again, no response is forthcoming. There is no contingency plan. I can't even sleep in my car, as I've left the keys in Ben's house for safekeeping.

Finally, I see some movement through the frosted glass pane, and a bleary eyed Ben staggers along the hallway. He had dozed off in front of the telly, and was in a state of deep slumber. It doesn't take me long to fill him in on the highlights of the evening, as there weren't any. He shows me to my quarters, and I carefully set my alarm for 4.30am.

Just three and a half hours later, my watch dutifully bleeps and I severely chastise myself for being such a stupid git. I should be two hundred miles south of here, and I should be tucked up in bed with my wife, assured of two more hours of sleep. Instead, I have to crawl out from under the warm duvet; dress immediately; forego breakfast, and slink out to my car in the darkness. I'm determined to reach school on time, and by five o'clock I'm already hurtling down the M6, well ahead of schedule. The toll road is completely clear and it even seems as if I'll have time to pop home for a shit, shave, shower and Shreddies. Everything is going wonderfully well until all of the other early-bird commuters come out of the woodwork near Luton, and I grind to a halt. It is now touch and go, so I am forced to head straight for school. It is 8.30am when I drive through the gates, and twenty minutes later I am teaching. I did it!

Ben was right. The plan *was* foolproof. So why do I feel such a fool?

COMPANION 10

Name: Dave Coward
Birthplace: Hull
Relationship: School friend
Allegiance: Hull City

Relevant History

Dave is my best mate, but we started out as bitter rivals – rivals in the North Hull Cubs League. While I turned out for the Marist pack, Dave represented the Holy Name. A sizeable crowd of at least twenty Mums and Dads were drawn to the local catholic derby of 1973. The Marist won 3-1 and we went on to take the league title without losing a game, a feat that was sadly overlooked by the world's media when Arsenal emulated our achievement in the 2003-04 season. I was the league's top scorer with 38 goals, but Hull City's flawed scouting network typically failed to snap me up.

The reality was, that the North Hull Cubs League was not exactly a hotbed of future international talent. A good eighty percent of the participants possessed little or no co-ordination and only turned up out of duty to Lord Baden Powell. I didn't realise this at the time of course, and I thought that I was brilliant.

The next season, it was back to Earth with a bump. Dave and I joined forces to compete for our school side, which was crap, largely thanks to our inept coach, Mr Wildman, who employed the motivational tactic of pre-warning players about their impending half time substitution – the day before the game. Therefore, regardless of whether or not he was playing a blinder, Dave was often removed from the fray at the break, to be replaced by Jeffrey; an enthusiastic but scraggy and ineffective misfit who, irritatingly, always showed up at training and won his place on the bench out of pure sympathy. Consequently, promising half-time situations were frequently turned into cricket-score defeats, but Wildman the 'Tinkerman' persevered with his policy. They were frustrating times for Dave and I, following the glory days of the Cubs league, but our united suffering helped to cement a long and lasting friendship.

When it came to the support of our local teams, Dave was definitely more passionate about rugby than football. In 1980, Rugby League was big in Hull. Quite simply, we boasted the best two sides in the country and on 3rd May they both made it all the way to the Challenge Cup Final at Wembley. In contrast, we rarely boasted about our football team and there was a grave danger that City were about to drop into Division Four for the first time in their history. In our penultimate game we needed a win at home to Southend to guarantee safety. Surely, the city would give the game its full backing and a huge crowd would turn out to roar us to victory. There was just one small snag. By a cruel twist of fate, the football league fixture computer had scheduled our crunch match for 3rd May. Most of the City of Hull were planning a little day out in London on that date, and the rest would be glued to Grandstand. It was a major test of loyalty. Dave headed for Wembley like a shot.

In its ignorance, the media infuriatingly labelled it 'The All Humberside Final'. As far as I was aware, neither Hull Kingston Rovers nor Hull F.C. had re-located to Scunthorpe, Grimsby or Immingham, so why on Earth the residents of North Lincolnshire were included in the party is beyond me. Would a Sheffield Wednesday v Sheffield United Cup Final be billed repeatedly as the all Yorkshire final? I doubt it.

It was a close, tense affair but the Robins finally came out on top with a 10-5 win. Unfortunately for the deserters, they missed a real treat at Boothferry Park. I've never actually seen any footage of Keith Edward's volley, but film must exist (maybe on a Bobby Robson coaching video) for in the 1990 World Cup quarter-final, Paul Gascoigne and David Platt managed to re-enact a carbon copy of it to defeat Belgium in the last minute of extra time. The Edwards wonder-strike settled the match; the crowd invaded the pitch, and the players saluted all 3,823 of us from the director's box – a vote of thanks for not buggering off to London. It felt just like promotion, I assumed: promotion being unexplored territory for any fans under the age of twenty.

Rugby became less of a distraction to Dave as Hull K.R.'s might diminished and today, thankfully, he is a regular visitor to the K.C. Stadium. It is a measure of City's recent progress that I must now contact Dave to guarantee safe possession of a ticket for home games in a 25 000 all-seated arena – a far cry from that desperate day against Southend, when they couldn't even give them away.

On my home visits, it has become a pre-match ritual for Dave and I to meet up the night before to sink a few beers at a local hostelry. Once there, we can quite happily talk serious, uninterrupted, undiluted, unrelenting football for the whole of the evening. The subsequent lack of opportunity for general chit-chat, inevitably leads to that awkward situation when I return home, as I get faced with the tricky question:

"How are Louise and the kids?"

I am forced to lie of course, and I immediately provide Dave's entire family with a clean bill of health. Dave meanwhile, carries out a parallel diagnosis back at his house, and likewise, my family too are all passed fit.

The Tigers fixture list has always been carefully scrutinised before trips home, and Dave has followed the same procedure for journeys south. Back in 1986, before the complications of wives and children, I was residing in Barnet in North London and Dave made two memorable visits; memorable for very different reasons.

In our youth (well, early twenties), we were either undeniably brave or bloody stupid, because we chose Millwall for our first outing. The Tigers v The Lions. With hooliganism at its peak, and English clubs banned from Europe, Millwall fans had developed a well-deserved reputation as the biggest bunch of nutters in the league. We travelled in disguise.

There was no problem getting *into* the ground, but it was the getting *out* that worried us, and when Frankie Bunn struck the winner two minutes from time, he inadvertently reduced our chances of returning to Barnet alive. In such situations, it was customary for Millwall fans to rip up the seats and aim them at our heads but clearly, most of these had already been removed. Instead, we observed through the protective wire fencing, hundreds of mad-eyed meat-heads chanting songs which explicitly described our method of death. We were trapped in the Lion's Den.

On our eventual release, we felt more like wildebeest than Tigers. A number of mental lions were stalking our herd, waiting to pick off the weakest link. Dave and I felt vulnerable. We knew that at some point we would have to break ranks and make a bid for the tube station. The alternative, and possibly the safer and more sensible option, was to board the convoy of Hull-bound coaches and end up at a drizzly Ferensway at two o'clock in the morning – tempting. We asked the advice of a policeman. His wise words proved to be invaluable.

"Just keep your mouths shut and you should make it."

And make it we did – all the way back to Barnet for last orders in the Pizza Hut. It was the icing on the cake for a perfect evening's entertainment.

Following the highly successful expedition to the Den, we tried for a repeat experience in December. Selhurst Park was the destination on this occasion and Crystal Palace were to be our victims. The weekend began very well. We opted to hit the Pizza Hut on the Friday night this time around, and we were joined by two Peters: my brother and my flatmate.

Flatmate Peter was a Spurs fan, and even though I had gamely accompanied him to watch Waddle, Hazard, Falco & co. on several occasions, he refused to waste his hard earned dough on someone else's team, and we were unable to persuade him to attend the match.

During our meal, it became apparent that Dave wasn't feeling too good, and although we all obviously expressed our deep concern, it didn't stop us from sharing out his unwanted pizza. By the time we had returned to the flat he was looking as white as a sheet, with a hint of green. We all turned in early, in the hope that a good night's kip would cure Dave of his mystery bug. I didn't feel great either, but that was down to eating 33 percent more pizza than planned.

Any mystery surrounding Dave's illness was blown away during the night, as the whole street was kept awake by the echoes of his retching. Another of my flatmates, Lesley, played the Florence Nightingale role through the hours of darkness and patiently tended to his needs – the main need being to empty a sick bucket every half an hour.

By daybreak, the last dribbles of bile had been ejected from Dave's body and he was talking in positive terms about making it to the match. But then, as the two Peters and I started to fry up our full English breakfast, he seemed to change his mind again and his close friendship with the toilet bowl was re-established. Once more, we sympathised with poor Dave as we shared out his bacon.

Our plan was to set off at eleven o'clock, so Dave had to undergo a late fitness test. The aroma of our elevenses coffee and chocolate biscuits made him heave again but no vomit was forthcoming, so he was duly passed fit. We made for High Barnet tube station and started the journey to South London. Every five minutes Dave clutched his stomach and doubled over in pain. As we headed further into London, the train became more crowded but at least we knew that Dave's guts were well and truly drained and the worst-case scenario would be a spot of unproductive strained retching. Other passengers would adopt the traditional British reaction of looking the other way, in the belief that they had selected the carriage with the nutter.

Upon reaching Waterloo station, Dave's contractions were becoming more frequent and our jokes about fetching hot water and towels were not going down very well. The mix of smells from fast food outlets were more than Dave could take, and he eventually sat down on the platform like the archetypal wounded soldier urging us to go on without him.

"Leave me here," he groaned. "You'll stand more of a chance on your own."

Peter and I looked at each other. It was a brave selfless act on Dave's part, but we both instinctively knew what we must do.

"OK Dave. Hope you get home alright. We'll phone you tonight with a match report."

I think Dave had been watching too many war films, where the dogged and loyal comrades carry the injured party to safety. No chance. We said our good-byes and followed our noses towards the alluring whiff of the nearest burger bar. Dave headed for King's Cross, spurred on by the thought of a speedy train back to Hull, and the opportunity to curl up and die in the comfort of his own bed.

We later regretted our lack of compassion as City were well and truly trounced 5-1 by a rampant Palace side containing a little known strike partnership of Mark Bright and Ian Wright. A bit like Ant and Dec, most people were not really sure which one was which, although I confidently predicted that the pacier Wright would one day play for England. We completely failed to spot his potential as a future chat show host and presenter of the National Lottery.

It turned out that Dave was suffering from a gastric problem similar to irritable bowel syndrome – except it affects his stomach. He goes through the same ordeal about three times a year on average. It is often linked to people who support inconsistent football teams and sufferers are commonly deemed to be, 'Sick as a Parrot'.

VENUE 10 – THE MADEJSKI STADIUM

Reading 3 Hull City 1

Saturday 19th November 2005 – 3pm

Dave is in good health when he arrives in Hemel Hempstead on the Friday night, so we decide not to tempt fate by visiting the Pizza Hut. Instead, we go for the Chinese take-away option, followed by a few beers at the local. It is a bitterly cold evening and temperatures have dipped to minus four. By midnight, a heavy frost has already formed on the cars and we are thankful that Reading no longer play at Elm Park, where a lack of under soil heating would surely have resulted in postponement.

We awake on Saturday to see that Jack Frost has continued his hard work throughout the night. Several layers of clothing will be required for today's outing, and it's hard to believe that only one calendar month has passed since the tropical day at Southampton.

Despite the icy weather, the M25 and M4 are trouble-free, and we make it to Reading within the hour. There is plenty of time to spare so we drive straight past the impressive Madejski Stadium and begin the search for a suitable pub, but this proves to be an almost impossible challenge. The stadium seems to be sited in the middle of an enormous industrial estate, and the only visible buildings are warehouses and retail parks. I'm reluctant to venture into the town centre so we settle for nearby McDonalds, which is teeming with supporters from both sides.

We devour our burgers outside, whilst admiring the view of the Madejski, which is built upon a raised plateau: not a natural geographical feature apparently, but an old landfill site. Overlooking the whole area a huge, almost surreal-looking, wind turbine. The air today is cold and still, so its giant blades are refusing to rotate, which could be a problem if the floodlights and under soil heating are relying on it.

The bar inside the stadium looks like our safest bet for a drink, so we begin the uphill march to the turnstiles. It's all mod cons here at Reading, and on arrival, we are asked to swipe our ticket underneath

bar code scanner, which activates the turnstile allowing us to enter. In theory, this should make the attendants at the gates redundant, but in practice, it makes them even more indispensable as they are needed to repeatedly give instructions to the clueless fans.

The Reading pub shortage means that the bar is extremely busy, and the brass monkeys weather ensures that everyone stays put until seconds before kick off. This results in a mass rush for the best unreserved seats at about 2.57pm, which is how Dave and I end up in the far left corner of the South Stand.

Reading have been in tremendous form recently, and they come out fighting. City don't know what has hit them, and they spend the first twenty minutes reeling on the ropes. We should be out for the count but Myhill is in inspired form, and despite their supremacy, the Royals manage only the one goal: a seventh minute breakaway strike from American international, Bobby Convey.

It takes us about half an hour to come to our senses, and in the closing stages of the half, we actually create some decent chances of our own. Leon Cort somehow blasts one at the keeper from point-blank range, and Barmby hits the post with a header. Encouraging signs.

Shortly before the interval, a young lady, weighed down with sound equipment, wanders up the aisle and parks herself in the vacant seat beside me. She leans across and asks me if we would mind being interviewed on Radio Humberside during the break. I find myself agreeing, before my icy brain can engage its gears, then I tell Dave what I've just let him in for.

The whistle goes, and everyone bolts for the bar to thaw out. Dave and I remain frozen to our seats while Amanda, the ace reporter, waits for the signal from her colleague high up in the press box. Eventually, she is given the go-ahead; a microphone is thrust into my face, and the questions come thick and fast. I know it's not exactly the World Service, but it's still live radio, and I'm suddenly conscious that if I say something stupid, there is no backtracking.

Inevitably, I'm asked what I think of the show so far, which is my cue to give a glowing reference to Bo Myhill, who has pulled off at least four world class saves to keep us in contention. Then, without being prompted, I give detailed accounts of the late chances for Cort and Barmby. I'm really rambling now, but Amanda is an experienced pro, and she tactfully cuts in to shut me up.

Dave is finally given his moment and she quizzes him about City's chances of a comeback. He astutely points out that Burgess is getting plenty of joy in the air, and that we just need to feed off his knockdowns.

The interview ends, and our suave double-act has made an accomplished radio debut – the new 'Saint and Greavsie,' perhaps. I soon realise, though, that we probably don't possess the necessary telepathic understanding for a lengthy career in the media, as Dave turns on me and says, "You bastard! You said everything that I was going to say!"

However, Dave's observations about Burgess being 'the key,' prove to be most prophetic. Ten minutes into the second half, the big centre forward meets Lynch's cross at the far post, and he nods across goal for Barmby to glance it home. We both agree, as we celebrate, that Radio Humberside must surely find a slot for its two new pundits. Not only have we provided an accurate and in-depth summary of the first half; we have also told them what will happen in the second half!

For a few heady minutes, we actually believe that City might pull off the win, and end Reading's twenty-match unbeaten run. Our brief period of over-optimism lasts for barely quarter of an hour, though, as Reading ruthlessly strike twice within a minute. Firstly, Doyle hooks in a volley via the underside of the bar, and then Convey sets off on another unstoppable run from midfield, before laying it inside for Little to waltz through the remaining defenders and stroke it in. Game over.

We thankfully manage to hold them to just the three. Lita blazes over a sitter from about six yards, and then Myhill produces another wonder save to keep out Little's header.

It has been an entertaining match, but we have been outclassed, and Reading look like promotion certainties. It is the Tigers fourth consecutive defeat, and we slip ominously into the bottom three. Just three weeks ago, I was seriously considering us for a place in the play-offs. It just goes to show that this is an extremely competitive division: there are no easy games, and we will have to scrap for every point.

COMPANION 11

Name: Anthony Collingwood
Birthplace: Paisley, Nr. Glasgow
Relationship: Brother
Allegiance: None

Relevant History

Tony is the only companion on my list with no affinity, whatsoever, for any team, whatsoever. Somewhere along the line, his footballing education came seriously off the rails: so much so, that by the age of twelve, he had totally rejected the sport.

And yet, it had all begun with such tremendous promise. An impressionable little seven year-old was unquestionably gripped along with the rest of the nation in 1966 when Bobby Moore lifted the World Cup and Sir Geoff completed that glorious hat trick. The interest was still genuine in 1970 as he obsessively collected the entire set of Esso coins for the Mexico tournament, and like the vast majority of normal young school children, he would fervently swap his precious football cards at any given opportunity on the playground. His impressive gift for reeling off the stars of the 1970-71 season stays with him even to this day. Peter Osgood, Terry Conroy, Cyril Knowles and the like, are names that are indelibly imprinted on his brain. Ask for any present-day players, however, and he draws a blank. To top it all, it was a golden era for the Tigers, with Chilton, Wagstaff and Butler threatening to lead us into the top flight for the first time ever.

But mysteriously, in 1971 the trail runs cold. Football had become an irrelevance, so the poor lost soul was forced to find alternative hobbies to fill the gigantic void left by its absence. Astronomy had always been a pretty fierce rival. The Apollo moon landings of the early seventies had really captured his imagination, and while my bedroom grotto was plastered with cuttings from 'Shoot', Tony's played host to a giant map of the moon. Armstrong and Aldrin had replaced Pele and Charlton in his affections. (That's Neil Armstrong of course; not George Armstrong of the 1971 Arsenal double winning side).

Stamp collecting, origami and model making all had a good run, and on days when the men of the house visited Boothferry Park, Tony would stay home to watch a black and white movie on BBC2 with Mum. Grandstand never got a look-in.

Another great passion was reading. He could quite happily lie on the sofa for hours on end, in mid summer, ploughing through voluminous novels such as 'Catch 22' or 'Lord of the Rings'. How could he possibly prefer that to a four-hour 2 v 2 game of football in the garden with his three brothers using jumpers for goalposts?

If he wasn't reading, then he would surely be drawing. Cartooning to be more precise. The family discovered at a very early stage, never to remain still for longer than five minutes at a time, or you were in grave danger of being seriously caricatured. All of our worst features would be grossly exaggerated and whereas, originally I had been blissfully unaware of my bulbous nose, beaky top lip and Jimmy Hill chin, I latterly transformed into a paranoid, camera shy hermit at all christenings, weddings and parties.

Back then, I felt quite sorry for him, but today I reluctantly accept, as he runs his own successful animation company, that the absent distraction of football has had a hugely positive effect on his life and career. Those thousands of hours spent reading and drawing have not been a total waste of time after all. Can the same conclusion be drawn from my thousands of hours playing football, watching football, discussing football and scrutinising the league tables in the Sunday newspapers? It is indeed a scary question and one that I decline to ponder, for I fear that I know the answer.

Whilst training to be an animator in the early 1980's, Tony resisted a golden opportunity to rediscover his Hull City roots. Despite studying in Beaconsfield, Buckinghamshire, he somehow contrived to flat share in

Kensington with fellow student and die-hard Tigers fan – Mark Herman. Mark's fanaticism had led him to co-write the classic football anthem, 'The Tigers are Back,' by 'The Amber and Black,' a single that shifted plenty of copies in the Hull area, but one that oddly failed to make a national impact. It was written together with Henry Priestman, a singer/songwriter who certainly did go on to achieve some national recognition, scoring a string of chart successes and two number one albums with 'The Christians'. Mark has also since hit the heights as a film director. 'Brassed Off' and 'Little Voice' brought him much acclaim and respect in the industry.

However, back in 1983, their early humble collaboration needed a boost from the Tigers new chairman, Don Robinson, a charismatic entrepreneur from Scarborough who joyfully wallowed in his local status as saviour of Hull City Football Club. Home games were often preceded by a 'lap of adulation' involving the hand out of various freebies to his loyal subjects. On one pre-match circuit, he nearly decapitated several fans with copies of Mark and Henry's record as he randomly hurled them at the faithful. The vinyl discs seared lethally out of their sleeves, and those who didn't lose their heads or eyes quite possibly lost their fingers in a vain attempt to fend off or even catch the razor-sharp gifts.

Another of his walkabouts was particularly reminiscent of a scene from Disney's Pinocchio, where hordes of greedy children arrive at Pleasure Island to sample a range of forbidden delights. Robinson, in his infinite wisdom, decided to throw hundreds of cigars into the lower terraces, most of which ended up in the curious little hands of the under six-teens. Naturally, they went straight round the back of the stand to light up. The passengers on the next train to arrive at Boothferry Halt must have been rubbing their eyes in disbelief at the sizeable colony of cigar-puffing youngsters crouched on Kempton's rear terrace.

Despite the 1985 resurgence, and eventual promotion under Robinson's influence, and Brian Horton's management, Tony failed to see the light. If anything, his incarceration with yet another Hull City nut turned him even more against the sport, and his footballing ignorance is now so great that he is too far removed from the game to even take the piss properly. His restricted knowledge of just the 1971 season does not provide him with a sufficient database to launch any credible attacks. This has forced him to rely on the oldest and cheapest shot of all; the line designed to infuriate football fanatics everywhere, for it shows up the perpetrator as a lost cause and sworn enemy of the beautiful game. You know the one. It will usually be delivered in a format similar to this:

"Football? Huh! A bunch of grown men chasing a lump of leather around a field?"

Oh yes, very clever. I could easily devalue his devaluation if I wanted to, just by devaluing *his* favourite pastime. Namely, drawing.

"Cartoons? Huh! A bunch of grown men using graphite filled sticks to childishly doodle all over re-constituted wood pulp?"

And while I'm at it, what about all those silly films he watches?

"Actors? Huh! Grown men and women prancing around in ridiculous costumes pretending to be someone else?" I could go on, but I fear that I may aggravate my stiff back if I continue to stoop so low.

So, why ask Tony along as my guest to a Hull City match here in 2005? Well, for entertainment value really, in the hope that he will come out with a number of highly amusing ignorant comments such as his classic recent goalkeeper gaffe. This was based on his vague memory of his one appearance at Boothferry Park back in 1972. The City keeper at the time, Ian McKechnie, had mentioned in an interview once that he was quite partial to oranges. Thereafter, it became common practice for the fans in Bunkers to shower the popular Scotsman with his favourite fruit as he took the field. Ian even used to come prepared with a small supply of paper bags, and he would neatly stack his rich pickings in the back of the net until half time. Some years later, this lasting image led Tony to ask the question, "Do they still throw oranges at goalkeepers?"

I'm sure there is plenty more where that came from.

VENUE 11 – LOFTUS ROAD

Queens Park Rangers 2 Hull City 2

Saturday 26th November 2005 – 3pm

My first task is to explain the constant restructuring of the football league divisions.

"Well Tony, we are now in the Championship, which is really the old Division Two. Two years ago, we were in Division Three, which is really the old Division Four, but is now League Two. We got promoted to Division Two, which became League One, but of course, is really Division Three. We then got promoted again to the Championship. If we go up again, we'll be in the Premiership, which is really Division One. It's quite simple really!"

Pleased that I have cleared that one up, we make tracks from his Wimbledon home towards the tube station. As we walk, it becomes apparent that Tony will be testing my patience all day with a favourite little game of his. I like to call it 'joke or jerk.' The rules are simple: he puts forward a number of ridiculous footballing statements or questions, and I have to decide whether they are true examples of ignorance, or deliberate attempts to wind me up. It's a clever game, but if it's to catch on in the East Yorkshire region, we'll have to change its name from 'joke or jerk,' as both words are pronounced the same.

His first effort is a real tough call. Having just explained to him that, nowadays, there are plenty of beer-serving bars in the league grounds, he asks if they also serve wine.

I truly hope that this is a joke, but just in case, I calmly remind him that we are going to a football match, not a wedding, and that the traditional pre-match tucker is beer and pies; not champagne and vol-au-vents.

Today's occasion has been hanging over Tony for some time. When I first broke it to him that he would have to endure ninety minutes of football, I generously granted him a choice of fixtures, and suggested that the Walkers' Stadium in Leicester might be an attractive venue. His reply was blunt and to the point, and it left me in no doubt about how ecstatic he was to be part of my scheme. "Look, I don't care about the stadium. It's like having surgery. I want to be in and out as quickly as possible. It doesn't matter what the operating theatre looks like."

Hence, the trip to QPR: crap ground, and it's just down the road.

Whilst sitting on the train, Tony dispels the myth that he couldn't give a toss, by pulling from his pocket, eight pages of trivia from the QPR website. The boy has actually been doing some homework. Granted, his chief motive was to check out the best pubs, but it's still an encouraging step forward. There is actually some interesting information in his printout, and a section entitled, 'What do QPR fans sing?' particularly amuses me.

Most of the lyrics are based on their intense hatred and jealousy of Chelsea, rather than the positive attributes of Rangers, except for one priceless ditty, which steals a classic tune from Mary Poppins. It relates to their 'no prisoners' defender, Dan Shittu, and it goes:

'Chim chim-enee, chim chim-enee, chim chim cheroo
Who needs Sol Campbell when we've got Shittu.'

The notes help to pass the time, and we are soon at White City tube station. Right next door, are the BBC studios. We walk straight into the main foyer to be greeted by our younger brother, Peter. He works in the White City offices, and is able to sign us in to the BBC Club Bar, which overlooks the Loftus Road ground (unfortunately not close enough to see the pitch).

We settle down for a welcome pint, and scan the room for famous faces from the telly. It's two o'clock, and we wonder if the football focus boys may soon be strolling in for their lunchtime break, but we are to be disappointed. As far as we can see, the clientele consists of a bunch of nobodies, much like ourselves, all desperately hoping to hob-nob with the rich and famous.

Peter and I are anxious to drink up and get to the ground, but Tony is quite relaxed, and he seems unconcerned by the march of time. For him, three o'clock on a Saturday is not the most significant moment of the week. He does not habitually synchronise his watch along with thousands of football fans across the nation, in the knowledge that the football league programme is just kicking off. His heart does not beat just that little bit faster. It depresses me to think, that two o'clock on a

Tuesday, or four o'clock on a Thursday will probably generate equal levels of excitement in Tony's world.

We finally prise him away, and stride quickly towards Loftus Road, passing unbelievable numbers of riot police along the way. The immense police presence is a slight over reaction to the unsavoury songs that some of our fans chanted during August's encounter at the K.C. Stadium. I had not heard these from my vantage point in the West Stand, but apparently they related to the recent London bombings, and there are rumours floating around on the Internet about QPR's intended retribution.

Consequently, thorough searches are being carried out at the gates, and the queues are lengthy. The frisking is then put on hold as an announcement initiates a minute's silence for George Best. This spontaneously turns into a minute's applause, which confuses the police and stewards, and they are uncertain about when to resume their duties.

We are allowed to pass, but underneath the School End, we are greeted by at least a hundred more policemen. They guide us along to the furthest entrance, but just as we see some daylight and catch a glimpse of the action, more police send us back down the steps, declaring that all the seats are taken (by police, probably). Many fans are becoming irate as we try to gain access to the stand, but the local constabulary offer no help whatsoever; no one is prepared to take the initiative, and there appears to be a distinct lack of leadership. It's easy to see how the Hillsborough disaster came about.

Finally…we are allowed in through the first entrance, which had initially been blocked off by a row of po-faced coppers. This brings us up onto the right hand side of the stand, which is full of vacant seats. Suddenly, we are spoilt for choice, but Tony's website notes are again of value. They point out that if you sit at the top of the upper tier, you can't actually see the whole of the near goal. Front row it is then.

We've missed the first eight minutes, but nothing much appears to have happened. The early exchanges are scrappy, and no one seems capable of holding onto the ball for longer than a couple of seconds. This leads to another of Tony's teasing questions.

"Are they only allowed three touches, like in Subbuteo?"

Definitely joke…I think.

It's time to fill Tony in on a couple of recent changes to football terminology. Firstly, I break the news to him that linesmen no longer exist, because in the interests of political correctness, they have been turned into 'referee's assistants.' This is thanks to just the one lady, who plies her trade on the touchline, so instead of calling her a lineswoman, the whole profession has been forced into a name change.

Postmen and firemen have suffered from similar initiatives over the years and have morphed into letter carriers and fire fighters. Thankfully, Postman Pat and Fireman Sam were exempt. Tony is relieved to hear that no football fan in the country has taken a blind bit of notice of this change, and it is only football commentators who seem contractually obliged to use it.

Another obsolete term is 'injury time.' This is now known as, 'time added on for stoppages,' which is a bit of a laugh, as we'd be playing until midnight if all stoppages were accounted for, especially those annoying late substitutions. Just as I am explaining this to Tony, a stoppage occurs. Myhill is forced to go and fetch the ball from near the corner flag, as the compact nature of Loftus Road has made ball boys redundant. I assume we are still allowed to call them ball boys, or has it changed to ball children or ball carriers or ball collectors...?

This little jog turns out to be Myhill's most strenuous act of the half. Rangers have not really tested him, and despite all their possession, it is City who have carved out the best chances. The singing subsides and the ground becomes eerily quiet. Shittu is suspended so we won't even be hearing any choruses of Chim chim-enee.

On forty minutes, though, we get something to cheer about. Fagan belts a long cross, deep into the Rangers box, and Ryan France rises like a springing gazelle to nod a powerful header past Simon Royce. As we leap about in celebration, everyone is turning to their neighbours to confirm that it was indeed Ryan France. Wow, even Chris Chilton would have been pleased with that one.

During the break, I do it again. I get ahead of myself. We've already got this one in the bag, and there are two home games coming up, followed by a trip to lowly Brighton. That could be four wins on the spin: we'll be looking at the play offs again.

Five minutes into the second half, Lynch sends another searching cross into the area. It finds the head of Billy Paynter, and it's 2-0. My half time dreams may yet become reality. Rangers have not looked like scoring yet, but even Tony knows that City have developed a legendary capability for self-destruction, and sure enough, the two-goal cushion soon evaporates.

The capitulation begins when the Hoops threaten to take a short corner. Three City players simultaneously rush over to thwart it, so the ball is hit long and Gary Ainsworth is left unmarked to head home. It's a soft goal from our point of view, and completely avoidable.

France very nearly puts us 3-1 up with an inspired solo run across the area, which ends with a delicate chip over Royce. It would have been a great goal, but a covering defender heads it off the line.

When you are down near the foot of the table, you tend not to get the breaks, and this is underlined shortly afterwards when a speculative 25-yard strike from Ainsworth takes a wicked deflection off Delaney's foot to loop cruelly over the stranded Myhill. Initially, Myhill's lack of movement convinces me that the ball is sailing harmlessly over the bar, and I can't believe it when the net bulges.

Rangers are really up for it now, and I fear the worst. It's backs to the wall, and the blue and white hooped shirts seem to be everywhere. It feels like we're playing Reading again.

Myhill's day then goes from bad to worse. He rushes to the edge of the area to gather a cross-field pass, but slips slightly as he gathers the ball. He lies motionless on top of the ball, legs and body outside the area. This inactivity arouses suspicion in the minds of the linesman and referee, and they jump to the conclusion that Myhill has got something to hide, and that the ball must have been fielded outside of the area. A free kick is awarded, and to add insult to injury, poor Bo is sent off. Matt Duke is the replacement but this means that we have to withdraw a player. Strikers are usually the ones to suffer in these situations, and it is Paynter who has to make way. Duke is immediately in the thick of the action, and he receives more touches in the final ten minutes than Myhill managed in the other eighty.

We enter stoppage time, and the Tigers make a rare foray into the Rangers half. A perfect opportunity to kill some time is then presented as the ball cannons up into our stand and the chap in front of me takes a clean catch. He is so pleased with himself that he thoughtlessly throws it straight back down to a QPR player, who takes a quick goal kick to set them up for a final assault. The wanabee goalie in front of me holds his head in his hands, and accepts the flack from his mates, who all make sure that he is well aware of his wanker status. When the final whistle eventually sounds, he wipes his sweaty brow, and heaves a great sigh of relief, thankful that he will not be credited with an assist for a QPR winner.

On the walk back to the tube, we begin to wonder if the police have called in extra reinforcements during the game. The ratio of coppers to fans seems ridiculous. The attendance is only 13 000, so our hosts will be lucky if there is anything left over from the gate receipts by the time they have paid off the boys in blue. Every twenty yards, now, we have to thread our way through banks of heavily padded and helmeted riot police, all standing like statues, eyes to the front, trying to look really hard.

Then, it happens. The first hint of trouble so far this season. We notice a highly suspicious gang of spotty youths crouched behind a wall, and as we pass, they all leap out and exercise their freshly broken voices with a mighty, "RAAAGGHH!"

"Are they hooligans?" asks Tony.

We're not sure. The police are not sure either. They hold their positions and look at each other, as if to say, "Shit! Trouble. What do we do now?"

Nothing, as it turns out. Nobody reacts to the provocation of the trainee hooligans, and they are all treated with disdain. The incident (if you can call it that) is over before it has begun, and we all continue on our way.

All in all, it's been an entertaining day and Tony has enjoyed it, although we are still some way short of a miraculous conversion. He took more photos of police horses than of the match, and he hasn't yet asked me about arrangements for our next game at Brighton. Oh well, one of these days, he'll see the light.

COMPANION 12

Name: Stephen McGeown
Birthplace: Johannesburg
Relationship: Cousin
Allegiance: Liverpool

Relevant History

Stephen's footballing loyalties are somewhat confused due to the nomadic nature of his early existence. He was born in South Africa, lived temporarily in Hull, and then settled in Hampshire, where the nearest team was an ailing Aldershot.

At regular intervals, he would return north to visit aunts, uncles and cousins, so I would take the chance to chip away with the Hull City indoctrination programme. At the tender, impressionable and gullible age of seven, he was ready for his first visit to Boothferry Park. Blackburn Rovers were the visitors on a cold December day. A resurgent Tigers side was packed with household names that just rolled off the tongue: Flounders, Bunn, Jobson, Skipper, Saville – the golden generation. It was all set up, but City failed to deliver, and so did the weather. It was dull and freezing, while the match was dull and goalless.

Stephen returned to Hampshire, where he resumed his distant love affair with the all-conquering Liverpool side.

He developed into a decent left-sided midfield player himself, before a recurring shoulder injury forced him to concentrate on athletics.

Now, aged 28, he is still involved as a club athlete, turning out regularly for Aldershot & Farnham District, where he is able to record an impressive 11.2 seconds over 100 metres.

The football bug lay dormant within Stephen for a number of years until the completion of the KC Stadium. Curiosity soon got the better of him, and he was tempted along to check out the Tigers new surroundings. Typically, he chose the Easter Saturday fixture against Northampton, which we lost 3-2, one of only three home defeats all season.

Nevertheless, he enjoyed the experience, and he sensibly realised that the Tigers are going places! His Hull roots were taking in water, and with a bit of careful nurturing, he could yet flower into a fully-fledged Hull City fan.

VENUE 12 – THE WITHDEAN STADIUM

Brighton 2 Hull City 1

Friday 16th December 2005 – 7.45pm

Allowing Stephen to drive will not go down as one of my most rational decisions. Half an hour into the journey, he reminds me that he took eight attempts to pass his test. I try to work out the reason for his string of failures as we swerve along the dark country lanes, two inches from the tail-lights of the car in front, but it's a real mystery.

One thing is for sure, I need a drink by the time we arrive at the Black Lion, which is situated on the edge of Brighton's 'park and ride' zone. This parking scheme is apparently the reason for the inconvenient Friday evening kick off. The festive season is upon us, and it was obviously felt that the combination of Christmas shoppers and seven thousand football goers would overload the car parks and bring the town to a Saturday standstill.

We are assured by the locals that the Withdean Stadium is just a twenty minute walk from here, so we settle down for a relaxing drink, and watch all of the Seagulls fans vacate the premises at least forty minutes before kick off. Slightly perturbing, but we decide to keep faith with our original intelligence reports, and stay put until exactly 7.25pm. At this point, Stephen unforgivably decides to visit the toilet, and he takes an absolute age. It's quite possible that he's taking a dump.

We are now in serious danger of missing the kick off, so we are left with no alternative; we'll have to run. I could really have done without this. Not only have I just speedily downed two pints of John Smith's, but I'm also wearing about five layers of clothing, and my pockets are weighed down with a camera, wallet, phone, coins and keys.

Despite stopping for a couple of brief breathers, we get to the ground on time, but another quick jog is needed to get to the City end. Just as we squeeze through the turnstile, a massive roar goes up. Someone has scored. We sprint down a long winding path and find ourselves at the back of a large bank of temporary seating. It is full of very happy City fans: we're 1-0 up. I curse Stephen for his untimely toilet stop but he blames me for being off the pace on our one-mile run.

After a few enquiries, I learn that Stuart Elliott was the scorer with a close range volley from Cort's knock down. I'm surprised that anyone can tell. With an eight-lane athletics track surrounding the pitch, we seem a long way from the action, and the far goal is just a speck in the distance. A pair of binoculars would be handy.

This is my first experience of a ground that doubles as an athletics stadium, so in one respect, it feels like I'm in Munich's Olympic Stadium, but in a hundred other respects, it doesn't. Adjacent to the back straight, sits another fragile temporary concoction of tin girders and scaffolding, while several private boxes and a large house/pub/pavilion type thing flank the home straight. There are no roofs on any of the stands to act as sounding boards for clapping and singing, and the atmosphere is not unlike a cricket match, as polite ripples of applause are offered up to the starry sky. The cold crisp weather is at least a blessing: the Brighton supporters must be hardened to the elements these days.

City are not actually playing all that well, but hey, we're winning, so everyone is in good voice, but I refuse to join in with one particular song.

"Jump up, if you're Hull City..."

Bearing in mind the flexible nature of the structure beneath us, I feel that this is not a good idea, but a thousand people around me are determined to discover just how temporary the stand actually is, and they wilfully jump up and down in unison.

After sixteen minutes, Brighton score, out of the blue. The troublesome Sebastian Carole works some space on the edge of the area and unleashes a dipping strike into the top corner. Now it's the turn of *their* fans to test the durability of the accommodation.

I'm becoming worried about the number of twenty-yard efforts that have flown past Myhill this season. So far, I've watched long-range shots find the net at Norwich, Southampton, Preston (twice), QPR and now Brighton. Is it Myhill's fault? Should the outfield players be closing down more effectively? Or are we just unlucky? I'll have to keep an eye on that one.

Barmby is unfortunate not to restore the lead minutes later with an excellent header, which the diving Blayney tips away at full stretch. Brighton then enjoy a good spell of pressure and squander a couple of decent chances, but we weather the mini storm, and I become increasingly confident that we will gain a result. However, just before the break, Charlie Oatway ruins my perception by planting an inch perfect curler into the top corner – from outside the box!

The referee blows his whistle just seconds after the restart to signal the halfway point in the contest. It also signals the halfway point in my season. I have now watched eleven and a half games out of the twenty-three, and it is time to reflect. (Two wins, three draws and six and a half defeats. Ten goals scored and eighteen conceded). It could have been better.

The second half of the season doesn't exactly get off to a blistering start either. Neither side really look like scoring, and the highlight of the evening comes when a rather portly looking gentleman is escorted along the track, right in front of the City fans. The chant goes up:

"Are you Prescott in disguise?"

The real John Prescott has recently given the long-awaited go-ahead for Brighton's new stadium and he is rumoured to be at the match. The Prescott look-alike milks his fifteen minutes of fame by waving and bowing at the City faithful, but he is rewarded with a predictable response:

"You fat bastard, you fat bastard..." He should have known better.

Our attention returns to the stalemate on the pitch. Stephen perceptively recognises that City have resorted to 'hit and hope,' but as the clock runs down, we dispense with the hope and just rely on the hit.

There are ten minutes left on the clock, though, when 'hope' makes a welcome return. Andy Dawson suddenly produces a rare surge of urgency as he dispossesses the Brighton defence and smacks a rising twenty-yard effort against the bar. Unfortunately, we have to wait the full ninety minutes before the rest of the team follow Dawson's lead. Four minutes of stoppage time are added, and finally, we punt a few high balls into the Brighton box to create a modicum of panic.

Two minutes left, and my phone goes off. It's my brother Mike, calling from his home in Madrid to get a match report. I explain that play is still going on, and I suddenly find myself beaming back live commentary to Spain as a big scramble ensues in the penalty area, but the ball will not drop kindly for us. The referee calls time, and the cheer of relief from Seagulls' fans carries all the way to the Spanish capital.

On the way out, we bump into Vin, an old school friend of Mike's. Vin now lives in Basingstoke (lucky lad) so the journey to tonight's game has not been too difficult. His car is right outside the ground, so he kindly saves us from another gruelling jog by offering us a lift to the Black Lion, where Stephen's car is waiting in the 'customers only' car park. I don't think this is how the park and ride scheme was meant to work.

It's eleven o'clock by the time we reach Stephen's hometown of Farnborough, and I am faced with a difficult decision. Do I crash out at Uncle Hughie's, or take a chance on the trains? I plump for the train and immediately regret it as the 23:15 to Waterloo appears to take a serpentine route through most of south-west London, stopping at every conceivable station on the way. I bail out at Vauxhall and take the tube to Euston, dashing up escalators and hurdling barriers, before surfacing at the mainline station. It is all to no avail. The Euston departure board is blank, except for one night train to Milton Keynes, which doesn't leave until 2am. Thankfully, it does at least stop at Hemel Hempstead, but I'm still forced to endure a chilly two-hour wait in a deserted railway station, where all the shops and food outlets have closed.

The night train, when it finally leaves, is filled with the strangest collection of people you could wish to see, and they're all drunk. The shouting, wailing and singing makes sleep impossible, which is just as well; I don't want to end up in Milton Keynes – well who does?

It is three o'clock, when I eventually collapse into my bed. It's the weekend, I've already broken up for my holidays and it's nearly Christmas, so I should be feeling content, but I'm not. Something is nagging away at the back of my mind. Now what is it?

Oh yeah, City lost!

COMPANION 13

Name: **Ray Coburn**
Birthplace: **Hull**
Relationship: **Ex Sunday League Manager**
Allegiance: **Hull City**

Relevant History

It's probably safe to say that Ray is the biggest football fanatic on my hit list. He must have spent a small fortune in recent years following City around the country; not to mention, the national side round Europe. He has been a regular at home matches since the late sixties and has held a season ticket since 1972.

This huge intake of football has not always been able to satisfy his hunger, and in the early 1980's, he felt compelled to found and run a football team of his very own. Haltemprice Football Club was born, and it spent most of its existence fluctuating between divisions 8 and 12 of the ridiculously enormous Hull Sunday League. The modest position in the East Riding hierarchy was of no concern to Ray. He just enjoyed the chance to play, and as captain, manager, founder, chief coach and kit washer, he was always guaranteed a place in the starting line up.

I would often help the cause by turning out as a 'ringer' whenever I came north for a holiday, but during the Easter period of 1986, I was to regret my Good Friday good deed. The attractive venue for the holiday clash with Durham Ox was Beverley Westwood. I hadn't even realised that there *were* any pitches on the Westwood, and neither had the resident cows; they had shat all over it.

The rough uneven pastureland was unfit for football, and the camber between ends was so great that the opposing goalkeepers only saw each other at half time when we exchanged ends. An extra challenge was provided by the gale force winds and driving rain that swept across the exposed hilltop. Captain Ray elected to kick against the hurricane, and a classic game of two halves ensued. Advancement beyond the half way line was viewed as a major achievement, and we were perfectly happy with a 4-1 half time deficit.

Early in the second half, I received confirmation that getting out of bed that morning had been a mistake. An opposing defender clattered into my left calf (long after the ball had gone) and sent me spinning into the air. Instead of landing safely on a soft bed of freshly laid cow dung, I was met by the raised elbow of the kamikaze defender, which dug deep into my left kidney. The wind was well and truly knocked out of my sails, and the pain was unbearable. I lay groaning in the mud, unable to catch my breath. After a prolonged period of treatment, I decided to play on (as you do) despite the throbbing ache that was pulsing through the left side of my body.

We clawed it back to 4-4 and I even managed to score; direct from a corner, with a huge assist from the wind, but the dull ache would not subside. I desperately wanted to return home and lie down, but Ray was driving, it was Good Friday, and it was lunchtime, so we headed for the 'Push' in the centre of Beverley.

Admittedly, the alcohol did help to temporarily numb the pain, but it was a massive relief when I was finally dropped off in Hull, where I could crash out on the sofa in peace. Little did I know that the day's events had barely begun.

At five o'clock, I dragged my aching carcass to the toilet to relieve myself of the lunchtime beer, but I was in for a nasty shock. My urine was a thick dark red, and I nearly fainted in mid-pee.

Having deduced that all was not well with my internal organs, Dad was summonsed to the toilet bowl for a thorough inspection of my bladder contents. He agreed that this was not normal and got on the phone immediately to the Royal Infirmary. The diagnosis was a renal trauma (bruised kidney) and the advice was to 'get down here fast!'

After a brief examination, and an expectation to produce urine on demand, (still dark red) I was transferred to the renal unit in Sutton. There, I received a more thorough examination: a bit too thorough for my liking!

Stripped naked, and presented with a fetching back-to-front surgical gown, I was left alone in a small side ward to think my own morbid thoughts. Eventually, an Asian doctor with a limited command of English burst in and uttered something that sounded worryingly like: "I'm just going to inspect your back passage with my finger." Naturally, I asked if he would run that one by me again.

"I'm just going to inspect your back passage with my finger," he repeated, as he snapped on the latex gloves.

"But we've only just met!"

I rolled over obediently and bit the pillow as his finger probed around: at least...I think it was his finger! It was the most uncomfortable feeling, and I made a conscious decision never to turn gay.

The rest of the night was even more uncomfortable. The violated arsehole was the least of my worries as the dull ache in my kidney turned into a dull pain, and the dull pain turned into intense suffering. By 6am, I was in agony and was violently sick into a bedpan. A doctor was finally called and I was informed that the blood was probably clotting in the kidney, so he prepared a large syringe with a blood-thinning remedy. Where did he want to inject it? In my arse! For the second time since my arrival, I was required to bare my buttocks, but this time I didn't mind.

Thankfully, the injection did the trick, and it had the dual effect of sending me off into a deep sleep. It was three hours before I gradually began to awaken, but now I felt strangely contented and the pain had gone away. My eyes slowly opened, and I received another shock. A priest was leaning over me, wearing a worried frown.

"Bloody hell," I thought, "he's come to administer the last rites!"

But Fr. O'Connor was the hospital chaplain, and he was routinely doing his rounds.

Later, on that Easter Saturday, Ray and a couple of the lads popped in to cheer me up, bringing a four-pack of Stones Bitter. I don't think they'd quite comprehended the severity of the kidney situation. I remained in hospital for ten days and was only allowed to drink water.

In subsequent seasons, I wasn't quite so quick to answer Ray's calls, and I would probably have lost touch with him if I didn't keep meeting him at every Hull City away match that I attend.

VENUE 13 – THE ALEXANDRA STADIUM

Crewe Alexandra 2 Hull City 2

Monday 26th December 2005 – 3pm

What a bargain! If you ask me, £3.50 is a small price to pay for the opportunity to by-pass Birmingham. I'm just throwing the correct assortment of coins into a collecting net at the M6 Toll barrier, when Ray phones. He has already arrived in Crewe, and has taken root at the bar of an Irish pub called Clancy's, close to Gresty Road. I should have no trouble remembering that one; Clancy is my wife's maiden name.

An hour later, and I'm there. Ray has advised me to use the railway station car park, which is virtually empty due to the lack of trains on Boxing Day. Refreshingly, no one has exploited the situation; the barriers are left up and the parking is free. Excellent, now I just need to remember the name of the pub.

Clancy's is just around the corner, and I sidle past the four beefy bouncers on the door unchallenged. The pub is modern and spacious, and a giant screen is displaying the dour midday clash between Charlton and Arsenal. Initially, the place appears to be well prepared for lucrative match day gatherings, but when I arrive at the crowded bar, I discover that there are only two barmaids in attendance. It takes me twenty minutes to get a drink. Bewildering.

Ray has teamed up with two more companions: Shane (another City die-hard) and Eddie, a resident of Crewe who supports Coventry. Eddie turns out to be a fountain of knowledge on all Crewe-related matters, and we are tipped off about their next crop of saleable talent. It is no secret, nationally, that Crewe are a selling club, and Dario Gradi has recently been singing the praises of Steve Jones and David Vaughan; touting them as future stars of the Premiership. The locals must wish that Gradi would keep his big gob shut, in the hope that, one of these days, the successful products of the youth system might stick together to form a promotion winning side.

Eddie's six-year old son is already a regular attendee within Crewe's extensive network of junior soccer schools. Gradi and the club personally monitor the development of talented youngsters, and those with obvious potential are often taken aside for specialist training. Such schemes are the bedrock of the club. They will never be able to afford big money signings, and the 'grow your own' policy is the only way forward. The sad reality is; they've been punching above their weight for a number of years now, and the likelihood of reaching the top flight must be slim at best.

We stumble out of the pub at 2.30, and are drawn straight towards the convenient fish and chip shop opposite, which has no queue. Things are going unbelievably well so far: free parking, great pub and handy chippie; all on the corner of Gresty Road, just a hundred yards from the ground. At this rate, we may even win today!

In a sad attempt to make their home sound more impressive, Crewe have changed its name from Gresty Road to the Alexandra Stadium, but the little ploy cannot disguise the fact that it's a shit-hole. Admittedly, they do have one decent stand, which runs the length of the southern touchline, but the rest is old and pokey, and with average gates of less than seven thousand, there is little incentive for further development.

A few Tigers fans have congregated behind the goal to the east, but the majority of us have packed out the North Stand, not because we have brought an unusually large following, but because it only contains eleven rows of seats.

The atmosphere builds as the players line up for kick off, and our excitable gathering bursts into song:

"We are `ull, we are `ull, we are `ull,

We are `ull, we are `ull, we are `uuu-ull..."

Ray and I look across at Eddie. We suspect that he is more of a Crewe fan than he's making out, and this provides an early test. He is not singing, and we refuse to buy his excuse that he doesn't know the words.

The early indications show that Crewe are technically very good, but a bit lightweight, and it is the Tigers who look the more threatening. Ellison has an effort cleared off the line and we begin to assert our authority. A bizarre misunderstanding then provides the Alex with a gift opener. Cort and France must have been bored by their inactivity as they both decide to compete for the same ball on the edge of the box. Their aerial clash causes the ball to drop kindly for the unchallenged Eddie Johnson, who provides a swift example of perfect volleying technique by lashing the ball into the bottom corner of the net – yet another strike from outside the area!

There's no need to panic though. City continue to impress, and it's not long until we're level. Ellison's deep cross is flicked towards goal by Delaney, and Fagan turns it in. Finally, some Christmas cheer!

It's just looking like the sides will go in level at the break, when David Vaughan conjures up some magic to get the 'kerching' noises ringing in Gradi's ears. He completely skins France with a sudden burst of pace, and delivers a teasing pass across the face of goal, which is just begging to be finished off. Gary Roberts duly obliges.

Ray, the eternal optimist, predicts during the interval that we will win 4-2. Honestly, after all these years, you really would expect him to know better.

In the second half, the game begins to follow a similar pattern to last week's Brighton encounter: the opposition don't look that strong, but we seem incapable of breaking them down. Peter Taylor is clearly thinking the same, so with three-quarters of the game gone, he gambles on a triple substitution. On come Paynter, Barmby and Elliott, and off go Andrews, Price and Fagan. Ellison switches to the right, and Elliott patrols the left.

The dangerous Vaughan appears to be the chief beneficiary of this reorganisation, as he suddenly finds that no one is marking him, and he begins to pull all the strings. He flashes a couple of shots at goal, sets up a host of chances, and generally runs at our beleaguered defence with pace and menace.

Eventually, with ten minutes left to play, his industry appears to pay off as he creates an opening for Roberts. Myhill parries the cross-shot, but Varney pounces to stroke in the rebound. However, just as I am facing up to the prospect of another defeat, the linesman raises his flag and the goal is ruled out for offside.

A spontaneous roar of encouragement bellows out from the North Stand as we urge the Tigers to capitalise on this fortunate reprieve. We are rewarded with an instant response. Billy Paynter intercepts a weak Crewe clearance, and tries his luck with a thumping 30-yard drive. Lady luck is now firmly on our side. Ten days ago at the Withdean, a similar Andy Dawson effort struck the bar and flew over. Paynter's attempt hits the bar and flies under...and in. It will surely be remembered as one of the goals of the season.

The impetus is now with City. It's as if someone has waved a magic wand and an avalanche of goals appears to be imminent. Ray keeps reminding me of his half time prediction, which now seems like a good shout. Perhaps the lad is not barking mad after all.

With five minutes remaining, Barmby is unlucky not to put us ahead. His low shot squeezes under the keeper and trickles towards the goal, but it runs out of steam a foot short. Paynter then nearly gets his second with a looping header that forces a great one-handed diving save from Turnbull. But, it's Elliott who possibly misses the best chance as he fails to connect with France's pinpoint cross, so we are deprived of the opportunity to sing that seasonal classic:

"Jingle bells, jingle bells, jingle all the way,

Oh what fun it is to see Hull City win away, hey!"

Repeat.

Oh well, maybe next Christmas.

COMPANION 14

Name: Dave Ledger
Birthplace: Hull
Relationship: School friend
Allegiance: Hull City

Relevant History

From 1972-77, Hull City were the most reliably inconsistent side in Division Two and permanently hovered around in a mid table comfort zone. The 1977-78 season bucked the trend and we became far more consistent. Consequently, by March, we were rooted to the foot of the table and were dead certs for relegation. Crowds dwindled as the below average crop of players produced their consistently below average performances. We were relying on the likes of Dave Sunley to provide the goals that would dig us out of trouble, and he was clearly not in possession of a spade.

The impending doom was too much for my Dad and he deserted the sinking ship. He had been threatening this for many years. His standard response as he trudged back along North Road following each Saturday afternoon let down would be – "Never again." Not the most original of catchphrases and one that he certainly did not own exclusive rights to. Previously, City had always managed to pull off a timely away win to trick him back into the fold, but this season we were being consistent, so such freak results had dried up. He really meant it this time and I would have to find alternative means of transport if I was to continue my loyal support.

The alternative was the bus, with Dave Ledger. Dave was my only other classmate at the time that went to City, so we made arrangements to meet up on the 14F. I would get on at the top of Greenwood Avenue, and he would board further down, just before it snaked its way through Orchard Park. This was to be the routine for the next season and a half.

Dave was a mild mannered, inoffensive young chap, but he used to undergo an inexplicable metamorphosis upon reaching the Kempton terraces; a sort of fifteen year old's equivalent of road rage. Nobody was safe from his hostile volleys of abuse: the ref, the linesman, the opposition, Dave Sunley of course, and anyone unfortunate enough to catch his eye. Many innocent bystanders have received the full force of his ranting as if everything was their fault.

Dave's Jeckyl and Hyde character is nicely illustrated by an incident occurring on his Ibiza holiday in the summer of 1984, (that's just a couple of months after City's 2-0 win at Burnley had left them one agonising goal short of promotion), so he was still a little bit on edge as he attempted to convalesce in the Spanish sun along with his gang of work mates. They crossed paths with another group of holidaying northerners one evening and the introductory dialogue between Dave and one unsuspecting Lancastrian went something like this:

"Where are you from, mate?" the stranger politely enquired.

"Hull. Where are you from?" replied Dave.

"Burnley."

"You bastard."

Thankfully, the guy had attended the crucial match and absolutely understood the reasoning behind Dave's surprisingly aggressive response, so a full-scale riot was avoided.

Our reliance on the buses ceased once Dave hit seventeen. He had left school the year before and his steady wage as an apprentice fitter allowed him to become the proud owner of a bright yellow, clapped out Ford Escort. We soon estimated that matches in the Yorkshire region should be within its range and made plans for an excursion to Bradford.

Three of us made the journey. Gary, another friend from school, was also keen to come. The car behaved, and Valley Parade was successfully found. We parked up, quite close to the venue in a street with a one in three gradient, on the slopes of the valley that lends its name to the ground. Dave assured us that his hand brake would be able to cope with the four-hour strain whilst it awaited our return.

We merged with the other black and amber arrivals and the police guided us through some very run down streets towards an uncovered stand at one end of the ground. It seemed that some long overdue regeneration was taking place in the area as we picked our way through a number of demolished buildings and piles of rubble. This was in the days before the Bradford fire disaster so there have been many more changes since. The view from inside the ground was not very impressive either. From our roofless, terraced embankment we could see the old, ill-fated, wooden stand to our right, whilst to our left, stood the smallest stand that I had ever seen at any football league ground. It did stretch the length of the ground, and it did have a roof on it, but it only extended back for about three steps. It was a bit like an elongated dugout. It wouldn't have looked out of place alongside the Subbuteo pitch in my front room.

During the course of the game, several footballs went AWOL over the top of the Subbuteo stand and undoubtedly continued to roll down into the valley for a couple of miles. It seems quite possible that the financial troubles experienced at Bradford in recent years could be due in part to expenditure on replacement footballs.

The game ended in a 0-0 draw, but the lack of incident on the pitch was soon to be counter-balanced by events off it. There we were, minding our own business, waiting to be shepherded back to our waiting vehicles, when without warning, a barrage of stones, rocks and bricks began to rain down on us from the skies above. We immediately equated that the best technique for avoiding 'sudden death' was to follow the path of each and every projectile so that appropriate evasive action could be taken.

One totally inebriated fan nearby, received a particularly nasty blow on his shoulder from a descending brick. His large intake of alcohol had completely shut down his reflexes, but at least it would serve to numb the pain. He probably woke up the next morning wondering where on Earth the big rectangular bruise had come from.

Some fans sought refuge by climbing over the high fencing onto the pitch, but the police were having none of it. They didn't appear to be as concerned as we were: presumably because they were on the safe side of the fence and wore helmets, while we were just the expendable away fans. Another explanation could be that they had seen it all before. Maybe this was the regular full-time routine and all the debris outside the stadium was specially shipped in each week to provide fresh ammunition.

There was a stubborn insistence that we remain on the terraces to act as cannon fodder, and this further fuelled my suspicions that they were all in on the little scam.

As I dodged the range of masonry, I couldn't help wondering just how much pleasure the Bradford fans could gain from their blind attack. Surely, half the fun of such an onslaught would be to actually see if your best shots were hitting their targets. It would be like ten-pin bowling with the lights off. Still, each to his own.

Eventually, the supply of ammo ran out and we were allowed to leave the ground, but there was still plenty of tension in the air of the surrounding streets as rival fans continued to chant antagonistic abuse at each other. We unanimously agreed to walk in the opposite direction, allowing us to enjoy a brief sight seeing tour of Bradford before returning to the car at a time less convenient to the hooligans.

Within twenty minutes, the area had cleared and we arrived back at the base of the street where our transport awaited. That was when we experienced our second shock. Only one solitary vehicle was visible as we gawped in disbelief up the steep slope. It wasn't an Escort and it wasn't yellow: it was a small van. The obvious check was duly carried out. Yes, this was definitely the correct road. A whole host of possibilities ran through our heads. Maybe the hand brake had failed and it had rolled down into the valley to join the lost footballs. Or had the Bradford fans recognised the Hull number plate and carried it off as a trophy? Or, far more likely, some opportunist sod had nicked it.

We paced slowly up the hill; Dave worrying about his pride and joy; Gary and I worrying about how the hell we were going to get home. As we approached the van, a tiny glint of yellow peeped out from the rear. To our overwhelming relief, it became obvious that Dave's car was safely nestled behind it. Without further ado, we climbed in and got out of town as quickly as Dave's balding wheels would carry us. As we made for the M62, I'm sure that I saw a lorry load of bricks pass by, heading back towards Valley Parade.

VENUE 14 – ELLAND ROAD

Leeds United 2 Hull City 0

Saturday 31st December 2005 – 12pm

For old time's sake, we agree that Dave must drive. The yellow Escort has long since been sold for scrap, and its replacement is a bottle green Mondeo, which looks more than capable of making it to Leeds and back.

An obvious advantage of the upgrade is the automatic windows, but this makes our old practice of hanging the scarves outside all the more precarious. One false flick from Dave on the control panel, and they could be lost forever on the hard shoulder of the M62. This was never a problem in the old Escort, where the only concern was whether the handle would come off in your hand whilst winding down.

Anyway, we have made the decision to come without scarves, foolishly believing the scare mongering from West Yorkshire Police that today's game will be accompanied by mass riots.

For a worrying spell, back in November, it had looked as though I might not make it to Elland Road at all. The award-winning misjudgement of the police had led to a hair-brain scheme, whereby Tigers fans would have to travel in an escorted convoy of official coaches from Hull City centre, directly to the Leeds ground. Nobody would be allowed to travel in any other way.

This would have led to a farcical predicament for southern, western and northern fans, who would have needed to by-pass Leeds to get to Hull, in order to get back to Leeds – all in time for a mid-day kick off. Then of course, after the game, they would be escorted back to Hull, before they could head west again to prepare for their New Year's Eve celebrations.

Quite rightly, Hull City Football Club refused to go along with these ridiculous proposals and threatened to forfeit our allocation in favour of a live beam-back to the K.C. Stadium. The police eventually relented, but our share of tickets was still limited to just 1 700. The capacity of

Elland Road is 40 242, so by rights, our ten percent entitlement should provide us with 4 024 seats – that's a shortfall of 2 324, for a crucial derby match.

Naturally, the small allocation has been quickly snapped up, although it includes a number of 'restricted view' seats, which sound a bit dodgy.

The back roads of Hull are snow-covered, icy and treacherous on the final day of 2005, but the main routes are clear, and by the time we reach Leeds, hardly any snow is in evidence. We follow some unofficial-looking homemade parking signs to the brow of a hill and end up in a disused timber yard. After forking out the customary five quid, we meticulously record the exact co-ordinates of Dave's parking spot, lest we should return later and suffer a repeat of the Bradford 'missing car' experience.

Freezing drizzle is sweeping in off the Pennines so we quickly head for the ground, where for the second time this season, we are required to negotiate a bar code system. At Reading, it had run smoothly, but not so today. Dave passes through without a hitch, but when it comes to my turn, the turnstile makes a quarter turn and then locks. I can't get through. Attempts to re-scan the ticket prove fruitless, so I desperately search around for a steward, although I'm worried that he'll accuse me of trying to pull a fast one.

Fortunately though, the temperamental turnstile appears to be an ongoing problem, and the advice is to squeeze through with the next punter. Typically, the next punter is a dead ringer for Johnny Vegas, and he also appears to be half cut, despite the early hour. He sympathises with my plight, but then proceeds to push his way through the big rotating gate, before I can fully leap in and join him. As a result, my foot gets caught underneath the bottom rung and we get stuck.

My newly acquired Siamese twin continues to push forcefully against the barrier, completely ignoring the subtle clues which are indicating a temporary fault: i.e. me, slapping him on the back shouting:

"Stop pushing you prat, my bleedin' foot's stuck!"

I eventually extricate my trainer, no thanks to him, and we tumble out of the other side. He picks himself up, dusts himself down, and waltzes off without so much as a backward glance. I begin to wonder if he actually realised that I'd been in there with him at all.

It's still only 11.15am. Dave and I are not hungry, so we go and check out the location of our seats. The Tiger contingent has been tucked away in the south eastern corner, and we are right near the back; just two rows from the very top. We have a poor view of the big screen in the opposite corner, but hey, we're not complaining: far down below, we spy an unfortunate chap who has clearly got a 'restricted view' seat. His nose is pressing up against a wide metal post, and the view is restricted to such an extent, that he can't actually see the pitch without leaning into somebody else's lap. I can't believe that Leeds have placed a seat in such a laughable spot – he'd have been better off at the K.C. watching the big screen.

We nip back down to the bar to warm up, and I spot a familiar face that I recognise from the Wolves game back in August. It's the crazy bloke who relentlessly sang his way through the entire match (or the 'Lead Singer,' as I dubbed him). At the moment he is dormant, but his throat is clearly being lubricated in readiness for the main event.

Dave and I return to our allotted seats in the stand, fearful that the 'obliterated view' victims might be on the prowl for something better. Within two minutes of taking our place, who should appear in front of us, but the 'Lead Singer.' He is instantly into his stride, but his songs appear to be directed towards his mates who have strategically spread themselves around the stand. It is highly likely therefore, that he is not in his designated seat, although it would take a brave man to explain this to him.

City are attacking towards us in the first half, and thanks to the 'Lead Singer' and his friends, there is no lack of atmosphere. Paynter crafts our first good opportunity. He's still brimming with confidence after his wonder-strike at Crewe as he cuts inside his man to flash a left footed drive narrowly over.

Leeds first chance of note doesn't arrive until the half hour mark when Lynch gets caught in possession in the centre circle to allow Robbie Blake a clear run on goal, but Myhill stands his ground to win the one on one battle.

We then miss a great chance to take a half time lead when Paynter fails to pass to the better-placed Fagan, and we are soon made to pay. The fourth official has signalled that there will be two extra minutes for stoppages, but it is three minutes later that Leeds score. I don't recall any stoppages during the time that was added on for stoppages. Douglas' low strike is a cruel blow as City have undoubtedly been the better side.

We beat a hasty retreat to the warmth of the bar area, where our frozen feet are treated to a fifteen minute thaw. It's nearly one o'clock, and the hunger is beginning to bite, but the queues are horrendous, so we settle for a packet of Maltesers from the vending machine.

In amongst the queues, there are a few sets of chairs and tables. It's the first time I've seen a seating area within a football ground bar. A few glum-faced fans have parked themselves here, and the late goal appears to have hit them hard, unless this is another section of 'restricted view' seats.

Time flies by too quickly and we steel ourselves for the second half, which is more than can be said for Hull City, who completely fail to turn up. It's all Leeds from the word go. Creswell hits the post as a warning, but the pressure eventually tells, when Douglas nods in his second after the ball has rebounded twice from the bar.

Despite the complete turn around in fortunes, the Tigers fans still keep their sense of humour, and they are quick to adapt song lyrics to reflect events on the pitch. Optimistically, we are singing:

"Three more, we only want three more,

So come on City score, we only want three more."

Just as we are in full cry, another Creswell effort deflects off Cort's outstretched foot, and loops over Myhill into the net. Without pausing for breath, the lyric changes to:

"Four more, we only want four more…"

But the referee disallows it for pushing, so we revert to:

"Three more…"

As we near full time, it is clear that City are unlikely to gain anything from the match, and Dave's terrace-rage tendencies come back to the surface. Not content with singing for goals, he takes matters into his own hands and screams out:

"For fuck's sake City, come on!"

But City already have their minds on next Tuesday's home clash with Sheffield United and it seems unlikely that they will be 'coming on' for the sake of fuck; the sake of goodness, or even for the sake of proverbial Pete.

The game fizzles out and we are left wondering how we can play so well in the first half, and so poorly in the second. When we get our act together and perform for the full ninety minutes, we should be a force to be reckoned with. As it stands, though, I am beginning to wonder if I will see another away win this season.

COMPANION 15

Name: Jon Hall
Birthplace: Dartford
Relationship: Work Colleague
Allegiance: Arsenal

Relevant History

Jon and I first met in 1989 when I secured a job as Head of PE in a Borehamwood middle school. Also on the staff, we had David Hall. David was only two years younger than Jon, but it still didn't prevent the pupils from branding them, 'Old Mr. Hall' and 'Young Mr. Hall.' Jon wasn't too fond of this, and he was even less amused when children believed the rumour that he was David's father.

Life didn't get any easier when David left. His replacement was a Mr. Paul Hall. Then, to bewilder staff even further, we employed another David Hall as a lab technician. Obviously, this was most confusing for some of our ill-informed, apathetic, stay-away parents, who would occasionally wander into a consultation evening asking to see Mr. Hall.

All of the Hall's helped out with my football teams. David was fanatical and technical; Paul was keen but clueless, and Jon was a disciple of George Graham's boring, boring Arsenal tactics. He was frequently spotted at after-school practices, training his flat back four to stand like statues and appeal for non-existent offsides. He greatly admired the endurance of the Gunners' ageing defensive line, despite the fact that they collectively provided stat-obsessed commentators with the opportunity to commit the biggest crime in football punditry – combining the ages.

Motty and gang would regularly overheat with excitement as they informed us that the combined age of the Arsenal defence was 134! Of course, in itself, this is a completely useless piece of information. Dividing it by four to find the average age would possibly bear some relevance, or if Tony Adams, on his own, was actually aged 134, that too would be a fact worth noting. But finding the sum total of their years on Earth seems like a pointless exercise.

Jon's addiction to Arsenal began with the 1971 FA Cup Final. Back in the seventies, this was the only club match to be given a live screening, so it could have a major impact on impressionable youngsters who had not yet sworn lifelong allegiance to any particular team. The Gunners won it in extra time with a memorable goal and distinctive celebration from Charlie George. He was hooked.

Jon has since realised that many other people have been similarly influenced. When training as a teacher in Dorset in the 1980's, he was puzzled by a preponderance of Ipswich fans in the area. The simple explanation, of course, was that their first cup final experience had been in 1978 – a 1-0 victory over Arsenal, ironically.

Bearing this rule in mind, it makes me realise that things could have been very different for Jon. The I971 FA Cup competition also saw a very successful run for Hull City, and I remember it well, as I went to three of the matches. We were fortunate enough to be drawn at home in every round, and we'd already seen off Charlton, Blackpool and Brentford, before being paired with Stoke. Waggy banged two early goals past a shell-shocked Gordon Banks and we looked well set for the semi-finals, but it wasn't to be. Stoke hit back, controversially, and won 3-2.

If only City had won, as we deserved to do, we would surely have brushed aside Arsenal in the semi-final, before crushing Liverpool at Wembley. Then, in all likelihood, Jon would have enrolled as a lifelong Tigers fan, and there would now be little pockets of 41 year-old Tigers dotted all across the land.

Teaching wise, Jon moved on in 1992, but we have always kept in touch, mainly through schools' football and cricket. We have both stayed in Hertfordshire, so it's been easy to link up for the odd fixture or two. We are still both going strong, and continue to show boundless energy and enthusiasm for school sports, which is incredible when you consider that our combined age is 83.

VENUE 15 – THE BRITANNIA STADIUM

Stoke City 0 Hull City 3

Saturday 21st January 2006 – 3pm

The Harvester restaurant is packed with Tigers and Potters fans, all enjoying a relaxing pre-match meal. A fair proportion of the diners are children, and a friendly family atmosphere prevails.

I can't help thinking that we have come a long way in the last twenty years. The Britannia Stadium is visible through the window, and I imagine that if this were 1986, fierce battles would now be raging in the surrounding streets, and instead of putting up the welcome signs, local pubs and shops would be boarding up the windows and battening down the hatches, in the same way that Florida's coastal towns prepare for an incoming hurricane.

The meal goes down a treat, and it's cheap too. When the bill arrives, I spot an interesting little footnote beneath the total. It reads:

"Why not treat your loved one to a Harvester meal on 14th February?"

"Because we're away at Millwall!!"

Having satisfied our stomachs, we wander across the road to satisfy our hunger for football. First stop is the programme vendor, and another £2.50 bites the dust. Yes, it's a bit steep, but there is no denying that the quality of programmes has greatly improved in recent times.

Before setting out, Jon had presented me with a 1973 programme for Hull City's Division Two fixture with Sunderland. It was dated 21st April – two weeks before their F.A. Cup Final victory over Leeds. The bargain price of the 24-page booklet was just 10p. Of particular interest, was an article on page three, which declared that adverts would soon have to be included, but they vowed that this would help to reduce costs.

Interestingly, today's Stoke programme contains over 20 adverts, yet still costs 25 times as much as the 1973 version. If all other products in the country had increased by the same rate of inflation, a Mars Bar would now cost £1.25.

A quick glance at the back page indicates that there is a John Halls in the Stoke line up. Jon muses how unbelievably funny it would be if his near namesake scored the winner. I can't see the joke myself. However, after scanning the manager's notes, we soon discover that Halls has just been sold to Reading, thus reducing his chances of getting on the score sheet.

We take our seats in the South Stand, and it is immediately noticeable that three corners of the ground are open to the elements, allowing the sunlight to stream through. The designers, though, have astutely noticed that the sun rarely shines from the north-east, so this is the only corner to contain seating.

Yet again, City begin well, and Jon Parkin very nearly gives us an early lead, forcing Steve Simonsen into a point bank save. It's my first viewing of 'the Beast,' (our new signing from Macclesfield) and it certainly seems as if he's well equipped to look after himself at this level. Having the build of a brick shit-house certainly helps.

We continue to apply pressure, and after just seven minutes, it pays off. A cleverly worked free kick releases Delaney down the left, and his deep cross finds Cort, whose firm header appears to cross the line. It bounces around like a pinball, and eventually hits the back of the net. I've no idea who scored, but Elliott seems to be getting all the hugs.

The lead is almost extended shortly afterwards when Jason Price swings his right boot from the edge of the box, but Simonsen tips it over. Jon is most impressed with City's flowing start, and I say nothing to dispel his assumption that we always play like this.

Predictably though, it can't last, and Stoke gradually gain a foothold. Collins' impetuous lunge allows Sidibe to bear down on the City goal, but Myhill beats away his cross-shot. It's generally a case of defending crosses and corners after this, and no further saves are required from England's future keeper.

Jon becomes excited by an article in the programme at half time, which carries a photo of Terry Neill (the ex-Tigers and Gunners manager). The piece is written by Terry Conroy, and it chiefly relates to that infamous 3-2 victory at Boothferry Park in 1971. At least Conroy admits that they cheated for one of the goals, and that if it hadn't been for Gordon Banks, they'd have been well and truly stuffed.

After this, Jon spends his time trying in vain to communicate with his 11 year-old daughter, via texts. He is desperate to discover the result of Arsenal's early game at Everton, and Rosie has been identified as the most likely source for the information.

Since birth, she has been subjected to an intensive programme of indoctrination, and she is now a devout Gooner, but no reply is forthcoming.

Out on the Britannia turf, a familiar story begins to emerge. Having dominated proceedings early on, we have now gone cold. Then, the linesman goes and gets ideas above his station by alerting the referee to a Collins tug in the area. The ref takes his word for it and awards a penalty. Typical; all we needed to do was keep it tight for the first ten.

The skilful Paul Gallagher steps up to take it, and hits it to Myhill's right, but our man guesses correctly and palms it away with a strong hand. This seems to spark off some trouble in the far north eastern corner. It's quite possible that some City fans have been rumbled following the penalty save. Reinforcements are called for!

Suddenly, an assortment of stewards and coppers bursts through the doors of a small brick hut in the south western corner, and proceeds to jog at a steady pre-set pace around the pitch towards the problem area. To sprint would create an impression of panic, and it is obvious that they have agreed in advance not to race, although one over-competitive steward appears to be breaking away from the chasing pack.

The City fans all give a sarcastic cheer as the comical gang pass behind the Stoke goal down beneath us. The atmosphere is really hotting up now, and it's about to get even hotter. Right on cue, Parkin adds a second with an amazing piece of Cruyff-like skill. It was at the 1974 World Cup that Johann Cruyff first executed his innovative turn, which left the football world gasping. Now, Parkin replicates it to perfection, right in front of goal, to set up a simple chance. He buries it, and the goading of the Stoke fans reaches new heights.

"We're just too good for you…" appears to be the favourite number.

It would almost have been worth taking a severe beating in the Stoke end, just to see their faces when Parkin hit the second, but we're not home and dry yet.

On 65 minutes, Collins (who has surely got Stoke down for a home win on his fixed odds coupon) clatters into Sweeney, and gives away another penalty. Luke Chadwick brushes Gallagher aside as if to say:

"I'll show you how to take a penalty; I used to play for Manchester United you know."

He cleverly dinks it down the middle, expecting Myhill to dive out of the way, but Myhill cleverly stays put, and the ball floats gently into his grateful arms.

"Myhill for England, Myhill for England!"

The afternoon is just getting better and better. Away to our right, the scoreboard shows that 75 minutes have elapsed.

"Fifteen minutes to hold out," Jon comments.

A stroppy bloke in front of us takes umbrage to Jon's negative George Graham influenced tactical instincts, and he retorts:

"Fifteen minutes to score a third you mean!"

We don't have long to wait. Fagan splits the Stoke defence with a sublime pass, which sends Darryl Duffy racing clear. He calmly strokes it home for the third. I hug the stroppy bloke and scream in his ear to congratulate him on his accurate insight.

"Duffy for Scotland, Duffy for Scotland!"

I've been waiting since October for an away victory, and with a three-goal cushion, I can really savour the last ten minutes. I notice a lady nearby who is also keen to seize the moment. She is taking a photo of the scoreboard, and I have to admit, it does look good – Stoke City 0-3 Hull City. I reach for my camera.

By full time, most of the Stoke fans have lost the will to live, and the large white 'Stoke City' letters on the North Stand seats are clearly visible. Outside the ground, we watch them trooping away like depressed zombies, and they fail to respond to the taunts of some fearless City youngsters who are furiously teasing them through three layers of extremely high fencing. Even if they had risen to the bait, conflict would not have been possible.

We pass two further indicators of the general home malaise as we circle the stadium on the way back to the Harvester. Firstly, we notice a lack of custom at the souvenir hut, where the proprietors are cutting their losses by shutting up shop early. Then, we come across the ticket office, which is selling tickets for the forthcoming FA Cup tie with Walsall. I count four people in the queue.

As we walk, I dutifully phone match reports to Dave in Hull and

Mike in Madrid, giving hoarse blow by blow accounts of all the drama. Jon is taken aback by my childlike euphoria and realises that he has been spoilt in recent seasons by Arsenal's team of all-conquering foreign imports. Sadly, he is unable to relate to the emotional mix of elation and relief that only come with unexpected away victories during season-long relegation battles.

Once in the pub, we link up with my old school friend, Gary, and his wife, Sandra. They had managed to blag some complimentary tickets, and had watched the game from high up in the best stand. Despite the privileged seats, Gary had almost managed to spark off another major incident, when he too, instinctively cheered Myhill's penalty save. Things got a little bit nasty, and there were heated exchanges, but there had been no need for intervention from the Keystone Cops.

John and I sup up and begin the two and a half hour drive back to Hemel, accompanied of course, by Alan Green. It's amazing how quickly the journey can fly by after a 3-0 win.

COMPANION 16

Name: Michael Collingwood
Birthplace: Glasgow
Relationship: Brother
Allegiance: Hull City

Relevant History

I am astounded that Mike has stuck with City over the years, as he is the archetypal fair weather supporter. This stems from his reluctance to accept defeat with any degree of humility, a trait that has impacted greatly on me throughout my childhood and beyond. My earliest memories of Mike's 'win at all costs' mentality relate to an innocent race in the park at the tender age of five. My elder brother, Tony (age 9) had challenged my father (age 44) to a race. Dad, calculating that his middle-aged legs were still up to the task, had accepted the challenge, so off they belted into the distance, leaving Mike and I to wage a secondary battle in their wake. I was the niftiest runner on my school's infant playground, so despite being two years his junior, I fancied my chances.

As we neared the agreed finishing tree, I was edging ahead and family glory beckoned, but my inexperience at this level was soon to tell. I had made the fatal mistake of running in the lane next to Mike on our imaginary track. I now realise that a space of three imaginary lanes is the minimum requirement in any race against my competitive sibling. The narrow gap between us meant that my lovely, warm, yellow balaclava was dangerously within his reach. In one swift movement, Mike whipped it off my head and threw it behind us. Unlike Dick Dastardly in Wacky

Races, his evil plan worked to perfection. I turned back to save the said balaclava, while he went on to take the chequered flag. At the time I was distraught, but as the years went by I became hardened and realised that resistance was futile. He was unbeatable.

The same scruples were evident in all sports, games and pastimes. You name it: Ludo, Cluedo, Draughts, Snakes & Ladders - the lot.

"I've never been beaten in a game of Monopoly," he would proudly boast. I truly believed for many years that I was just really, really crap at board games, until I reached the age of twelve and studied probability in school Maths lessons. This drew me to the revealing conclusion that it was statistically impossible for Mike to have acquired Park Lane and Mayfair in every game of Monopoly that we had ever played. Likewise, in Snakes & Ladders, his snake-free passages to the one hundred square were looking highly suspect.

As I grew older I learned to be more vigilant. I watched him like a hawk.

"Er...no Mike, you threw a nine there and if we just count that again I think you'll find that you should have indeed landed on my hotel. Five hundred pounds please!"

But rather like drug cheats in the Olympics, he would find new ways to keep one step ahead of the watchdogs. A game of Monopoly would be an exhausting affair. As well as trying to concentrate on my own game plan, I needed to be forever alert to spot new tricks, and they came thick and fast. Mike's sticky fingers would often glean a few notes too many from the bank. Community Chest and Chance cards had to be strictly vetted, as they always seemed to turn out in his favour. Every move had to be checked and double-checked. Refreshments of the liquid variety were strictly off limits during a game, as a trip to the toilet would leave the board at his mercy. But I still couldn't win. If ever a game began to swing in my favour, he would make his excuses and call it a draw. And of course, he always had the old favourite to fall back on should he find himself in a really tight corner: tipping up the board.

Auntie Gwen didn't help matters either. She worked for a market research company and every Christmas would send through the post the most popular new board game to have hit the shelves. One year, a game called 'Careers' arrived. An absolute Godsend for cheats everywhere. Mike cottoned on immediately and was soon into his stride, beating all comers. The old boast wasn't long in coming either. "I've never been beaten at a game of Careers."

Well, no, of course he hadn't. It was a game designed by cheats, in Cheat City, especially for cheats. The only way to beat him was to out-cheat him. This was how the game worked.

Players would make their way around the board, trying out different careers as they went; e.g. education, health, politics, acting etc. During your travels you had to collect twenty stars, which represented fame; twenty hearts – happiness, and £20 000 in cash.

The real beauty of this for Mike was that players had to secretly record their own progress in three columns on the provided little notepad. No one was allowed to look. Madness! Naturally, whenever I was within reach of my three targets, Mike would, metaphorically, remove my yellow balaclava, and reveal the magic figures on his pad. There was no way of counting back and checking results, so although his creative accounting was blatantly obvious, it was well nigh impossible to prove. When I think back now about that dubious secrecy rule, I can't actually remember ever reading anything about it in the instructions. It is highly likely that Mike invented it himself to further prolong his invincibility.

I gradually played less and less against him. The sliding scale of life therefore decreed that somebody else must play him more and more. That somebody was our little brother, Peter. The age gap was six years. Sadly, Peter was easy prey.

Perhaps the reason for Mike's admirable loyalty towards the Tigers can be explained by another aspect of his personality; his need to stand out from the crowd – to be different – to be awkward. If you supported City in the late 1970's or early 80's, it was embarrassingly easy to stand out from the crowd on Boothferry Park's sparsely populated terraces, and you were certainly classed as being different; some might say odd. Our meagre attendances of three and a half thousand constituted barely one percent of the total catchment area, so Mike could happily stroll around school, sporting his black and amber scarf, safe in the knowledge that he was one in a hundred.

His loyalty towards the Scottish football team did not enjoy such a strong bond. Along with brother Tony, Mike had been born in Glasgow in the early sixties. Dad had been relocated north of the border for five years before returning to Hull in 1962.

Mike liked the fact that he had been born in Glasgow. It was different, almost exotic, and it gave him an excuse to support a Scotland side that were arguably better than England throughout the seventies.

Then, towards the end of the decade, his need to be on the winning side superseded the need to be different. With Hull City, there had been no viable alternative for miles around, but in the international arena, Mike also qualified for England. Allegiance was rigorously tested during Scotland's inept 1978 World Cup campaign and his free transfer to the Sassenachs was conveniently completed a year later thanks to Kevin Keegan's sublime one-two with Trevor Brooking at Wembley. It was a convincing 3-1 victory over the old enemy and suddenly, Mike was an England fan. All traces of his errant past were erased. Posters of Kenny Dalglish and Joe Jordan disappeared from his bedroom wall and even the tartan rug was removed from the boot of Dad's car. We had our brother back!

Now passionately English and mad about the Tigers, Mike attended most of City's home matches in the late seventies. For many of the northern away games, we would join up with a noble band of followers known locally as the 'City Psychos' whose preferred mode of transport was a fleet of council double-decker buses. His commitment to the cause could not be questioned. In days when football violence was at its peak, you might say that driving into the heart of Bradford or Sheffield in whopping great blue and white Hull City Council buses might rank as complete suicide. Certainly, nobody in the higher echelons of the Psychos had carried out any risk assessments. The term 'sitting targets' springs to mind.

By the late eighties we both had to lend our support to the Tigers from afar; Mike from Malton, and I from Hertfordshire. City's fortunes though were once again on the slide and Mike's pre-programmed instinct to win at all costs was about to re-activate. He quit work and took up a job offer abroad; in Madrid, would you believe. Call me Mr. Cynical, but I did suspect a faint possibility here of a football related motive. He was about to swap the crumbling terraces of Boothferry, for the multi-tiered majesty of the Bernabeau. As 'Chance' cards go, this one had to be the pick of the pile.

Back in 1968 Mike had attended his first ever game of football. He sat on the very back row of Bunkers and enjoyed a comfortable 3-0 win against Huddersfield, although by his own admission, he gained more pleasure and excitement from the bag of Riley's Chocolate Toffee Rolls that Dad had purchased from the newsagents before the game. By 2003, he had arrived at that momentous occasion when he could take his own son to his first ever game of football, Real Madrid against Malaga. A 5-1 victory for the home side was witnessed by an 88,000 full house. No comparison really is there.

To his credit, Mike eagerly phones me at five o'clock every Saturday to receive an update on the Tigers fortunes. Yet, despite this commendable habit, it has concerned me for some time that his home visits have repeatedly failed to tie in with the Hull City fixture list, a cardinal sin for any self-respecting fan. His last game was an uneventful 0-0 draw with Swansea in 1994. It begs the question as to whether, for the last decade, his support has been purely superficial. We will see.

VENUE 16 – KENILWORTH ROAD

Luton Town 2 Hull City 3

Saturday 4th February 2006 – 3pm

Mike's flying visit from Madrid has given rise to a major family gathering in Hemel Hempstead. My three brothers, their wives, their offspring and my Mum have all converged for the weekend festivities, but only six of us are escaping to Luton, leaving just thirteen for Patsy to entertain.

Mike's old school friend, Vin, then arrives at midday to make it a round twenty for lunch. We don't linger for long, though, and we're soon girding our loins in readiness for the main event.

As we leave the house, Peter, my younger brother, produces a crumpled piece of paper containing scribbled directions to Kenilworth Road. Vin thanks Peter for his efforts, but suggests that maybe we should use his satellite navigation system. Peter sheepishly slips the notes back into his pocket.

Mike jumps in with me, as do Cristian and Stephen, our sons. Peter and his son, Kieran, decide to go with Vin in the satellite-guided vehicle. Peter's notes had strongly advised by-passing Luton and taking Junction 11 off the M1, but it doesn't take long for the superior satellite technology to overrule the pencil and paper method, and Vin's car obstinately veers off at Junction 10.

This takes us deep into Luton Town Centre (possibly off the satellite radar) and we get stuck in heavy traffic. I've no idea where we are going, so I am forced to drive without due care and attention in order to keep on Vin's tail.

We look out for any telltale match-day signs, which might lead us to the game: e.g. hordes of fans streaming in the same direction, police horses, distant floodlights or five pound car parks.

Actually, I already know that parking is going to be an issue, and when we finally hit the right part of town, the narrow streets only seem to offer places for permit holders. Mike winds down his window and asks a local bobby for assistance.

"Excuse me. Is there anywhere round here to park, which is not for permit holders?"

"You're `aving a laugh aren't you mate?"

His associate then ventures forward and suggests that we backtrack towards the Sainsbury's car park where we can legally park for the bargain fee of ... five pounds.

To save time, energy and petrol, we heed the advice and drive back out onto the main road, rejoining the queues of Saturday shoppers.

On the eventual walk to the ground, we receive our first hint that little Cristian is setting his expectations too high. It is a chilly day, and this prompts him to ask if the stands at Kenilworth Road contain heaters in the roofs, like at Real Madrid. I am about to tell him not to be so bloody stupid, when I remember that the poor boy is on the verge of a major culture shock, so I try to let him down gently with a non-committal answer, which vaguely hints that his young bollocks may indeed get frozen off.

Our back street route brings us out at a tatty old portercabin, which we soon recognise as the club shop. Its architectural attributes are certainly in keeping with the rest of the ground: i.e. it looks like it's about to fall down.

To reach the City end, we need to follow a narrow alleyway along the back of the executive boxes, where it becomes strikingly obvious that Luton Town Football Club just has to get out of here. With my arms outstretched, it is possible to touch the wall of the stand with my left hand, and the side of a house with my right hand. The place is totally hemmed in by terraced Victorian housing in the heart of a large Sikh community. There is absolutely no room for expansion.

Bill Tomlins, the Luton chairman, has been talking about relocating to a new site close to Junction 12 of the M1. A couple of years ago, they were talking about Junction 10. Maybe next year it will be Junction 14. At this rate, by 2020 they should be checking out sites in the Doncaster region.

The turnstiles at the Oak Road end provide further evidence of the ground's complete incarceration. They are actually built into the houses, and we can only enter the ground by passing beneath people's bedrooms and through their back gardens to a large iron staircase, which is adjoined to the rear of the stand.

From the top of the stairs, I spot a ball and some makeshift goalposts in a back yard, and I wonder if maybe this constitutes part of Luton's training facilities.

No sooner have we taken our seats behind the goal, than Stephen and Cristian request a wee wee. We return to the iron staircase and follow the signs to a toilet in the back of somebody's house, which worries me: we might well be trespassing. I am convinced that any minute, Mrs. Patel will appear out of a cubicle, knickers round her ankles, screaming at us to clear off before she calls the police.

We hastily make it back to our seats to soak up the pre-match entertainment, which is basically just a penalty shoot-out between Roary the Tiger and Harry the Hatter (who incidentally, looks a bit camp in his white nylon tights).

It is immediately obvious that this could prove to be a bit of a mismatch; not because of Harry's suspect sexuality, but because of Roary's football boots, which give him a distinct advantage over Harry's enormous pair of floppy size 23 shoes.

Roary goes first, and he blasts a perfect penalty into the back of the net. Harry doesn't even see it: probably because he can't actually see anything out of his ridiculously cumbersome foam head.

The roles are then reversed, and it's Harry's turn to try his luck from twelve yards. He swings his oversized boot like a giant golf putter and the ball smacks against a post. Yes! 1-0 Roary!

We're getting quite excited now, but with the next penalty, it becomes clear that the whole thing is a fix. Roary gently strokes his kick straight at Harry, and even *he* can't fail to make the save. Harry then inevitably equalises past the motionless tiger before running to his adoring fans for an exaggerated celebration.

We are then treated to a series of handshakes and backslaps between the two mascots in a phoney show of friendship and unity. Presumably, this wave of goodwill and sportsmanship is meant to sweep across the terraces, touching the hearts of all those who have come to bear witness. Yeah, right!

The real hostilities get under way, and Mike immediately gets into his stride, screaming and shouting at City's overworked defence, which is under the cosh from the word go. After just nine minutes Luton take the lead with Keith Keane's glancing header, and we fear the worst. They are running us ragged, and we could be in for a real spanking, which of course, will completely ruin tonight's family get together. We'll be a right trio of miserable bastards, and Tony (the black sheep – the one who doesn't like football) will be the only brother in good spirits. We tried to persuade him to come along, but he has done his one match for this century.

City are eventually given a sniff of goal with a free kick on the edge of the Luton box. In his ignorance, Mike asks:

"Who've we got who can hit one from here?"

Several people in the vicinity turn and glare at him as if to say:

"And where the fuck have you been since Stan McEwan left the club? Prison?"

It's another prime example of an out of touch Spanish exile that has been spoilt rotten on a diet of fancy Galacticos. Andrews blazes it over.

Shortly afterwards, the Tigers are presented with another free kick opportunity, but again, confusion seems to reign as players wander around aimlessly. Elliott mingles with the Luton wall, but then changes his mind and jogs back towards the ball, where he makes a sharp right turn. Andrews quickly flicks it across to him, and Elliott pings it into the bottom corner of the net.

The move has clearly come straight from the training ground and it makes a fool of the bloke behind us who had just bellowed:

"City, you don't know what the fuck you're doing!"

Clearly, they did.

The goal breathes new life into City, and suddenly, they are really up for it. Tackles are flying in everywhere, and Luton are no longer having things their own way. On 35 minutes, Elliott decides to use the springs that he secretly keeps in his heels to out jump two dithering Luton defenders. This creates the chance to cross, low and hard, into the six-yard box, where Darryl Duffy is the grateful recipient. 2-1.

This stokes up the choral banter between fans, which City instigate:

"One nil up, you fucked it up…"

Luton are riled by this, and refer back to last season's achievements:

"Champions! Champions! Champions!"

It's time for us to play our trump card with a well-known chant that has never been more relevant.

"Shit ground, no fans. Shit ground no fans."

It's impossible to argue with this one, but they still won't let go of last year's news, and they come back with:

"Shit ground, Champions! Shit ground, Champions!"

They are taking it all in good heart, until City score a third, and then they go quiet. The goal stems from an Ellison adrenaline surge (like the one he had at Southampton). He bursts powerfully past two Luton defenders like a runaway train, before cutting the ball back for Parkin to score. This gives rise to a few repetitions of:

"Feed the Beast and he will score..."

Attempts are then made to re-ignite the singing contest with the provocative taunt:

"We're just too good for you..." which remarkably, at this stage of the game, is absolutely true. There is no reply.

During the interval, Mike is buzzing. He has just rekindled (three times) the joy of bear hugging complete strangers during uncontrolled goal celebrations. In addition, he has spent the last 45 minutes screaming lots of very useful instructions at the City players, and he has now lost his voice, but this is not going to prevent him from barking out further helpful hints in the second half.

It is twelve years since Mike has sung his support for the Tigers from the terraces of a grotty football league ground, and he feels as though he has travelled back in time. This reminds him of the ancient document that he has brought along for our entertainment. From a back pocket, he produces his 1978 membership card for the Hull City Supporters Club, and the mug shot inside provides most of the Oak Road Stand with a good half time chuckle. His hair can only be described as 'wild,' and of course he is sporting the fashionable 1978 wing collars and giant tie knot.

Of greater interest, though, is the collection of autographs that surround the photo: Bruce Bannister, Stuart Croft, Roger DeVries, Mick Horswill, Malcolm Lord, Gordon Nisbet, and one more, which is undecipherable. Oh, the good old days! Mind you, today is a pretty good day as well; we're 3-1 up at Luton, and if we win this, it will go a long way towards securing Championship football for another season.

Much of the subsequent second half action takes place at the far end, where Myhill's goal enjoys a charmed life thanks to a succession of wayward shots and desperate blocks. In contrast, the City strikers rarely threaten the goal before us. A well-timed volley from Ellison is our best effort, but Beresford clutches onto it at the foot of the post.

Our two-goal cushion is maintained until four minutes from time when a diving header from Chris Coyne reduces the deficit. A nail-biting final five minutes have to be endured.

Again, the success of tonight's family bash is hanging in the balance. City's defence do their best to help our cause by punting several balls over the executive boxes into neighbouring gardens, but the ball boys have been stocked with an endless supply of replacements.

Deep into stoppage time, Elliott fluffs a regulation interception, which allows Carlos Edwards to launch a final raid down the right. My heart drops into my stomach as I get a flashback to last season when a similar attack down the right produced a cruel last minute winner. I scream at Elliott for his lapse of concentration: Mike tries to scream too, but nothing comes out. Edwards' cross is cleared, and the whistle finally blows.

Mike punches the air with delight as he realises just what he's been missing for the past eighteen years. Never mind Real Madrid, this is real football.

*****

"Well, that was the perfect weekend," Mike says, as we approach Luton Airport on Sunday evening. "Everything went according to plan."

But he is tempting fate. No sooner has he opened his big mouth than the radio informs us that all flights have been suspended out of Luton thanks to a small private jet, which has skidded off the runway.

Chaos reigns within the departure lobby, where everybody is frantically trying to make alternative arrangements. After a lengthy wait, Mike and family are finally able to reschedule their flights … for Tuesday morning.

Oh well, not to worry. We don't need much of an excuse to extend our weekend of celebration. We head back to Hemel Hempstead and crack open another bottle of wine to continue toasting the Tigers' entertaining 3-2 victory.

COMPANION 17

Name:	**Mick Hore**
Birthplace:	**St.Albans**
Relationship:	**College friend**
Allegiance:	**Chelsea**

Relevant History

Mick was witness to my most embarrassing moment. It was our first week at college and our first PE lecture. Thirty keen students were assembled in the gymnasium in their gleaming new college kit, all desperate to impress the gymnastics coach who stood before us in his 'Great Britain' tracksuit. Apparently, he had worked with the British squad prior to the 1980 Olympics, and it was quite clear that he didn't half fancy himself. My nerves intensified when Bill, the expert and mega-experienced coach, pulled me out from the group to assist with the first demonstration. He simply asked me to make a 'back' for a leap-frog, but in my state of nervous excitement, my brain mistakenly relayed this instruction to my ears as, "Could you make a backward leap-frog?"

"Strange request," I thought, "but I'll give it my best shot. This guy is used to the highest standards."

With cringing enthusiasm, I carefully lowered myself into a crouched position, before springing upwards and backwards, several times, like a demented frog in full retreat. But instead of a polite round of applause for my splendid effort, I was faced with stunned silence and a room full of quizzical looks. I sensed that something was wrong. Bill was as baffled as everyone else.

"What the hell are you doing?" he barked.

I hardly dared to give my answer.

"Er… a backward leap-frog??"

Uproar. For the next ten minutes, the group were unable to perform any further gymnastic manoeuvres due to their split sides, and when anyone did achieve partial recovery, it was only to imitate my spectacular misunderstanding. I was never going to live this one down. At least I had succeeded in one respect; I had made an early impression.

In the following weeks, Mick made sure that I received regular reminders of my blunder. As I routinely made my way around the college campus, repeated shouts came from all angles, "Hey Paul, show us your backward leapfrog." And it wasn't just Mick. Other members of the group would frequently request a repeat showing. But I could handle this. What I couldn't handle, were the complete strangers who got in on the act. It really pissed me off when people who I'd never met before, came up and asked for yet another re-enactment, as if I was some sort of performing seal. What response did they expect I wonder?

"Yes, sure, haven't you seen it yet? Gather round everyone. This is how I made a complete arse of myself."

No, I think my retort was usually more along the lines of… "And who the fuck are you?"

It took a while, but eventually people grew tired of hearing about the incident, although not as tired as me. Despite appearing to accept it all in my stride with great humour, I still bore a deep grudge, especially against Mick. His widespread broadcasting of the episode had damaged my street-cred before I'd even had the chance to build any up. I had to bide my time and wait patiently to exact some kind of revenge; and then Hull City were drawn at Chelsea in the FA Cup, (Mick's team). Could this present me with an early opportunity to take the Mick out of Mick. Certainly, the Tigers were the underdogs so I had nothing to lose, and nothing could top the humiliation of the backward leap-frog.

We travelled to the game together, but went our separate ways on arrival. Mick met up with some friends in the Shed, while I joined the City fans behind the opposite goal – a stand that has since been rebuilt and renamed – the Matthew Harding Stand.

In fact, the whole of Stamford Bridge has undergone quite a transformation since the early 1980's. Back then, there was a generous gap between the touchlines and the stands, and the vast open territories behind the goals were almost Wembley-like in their spaciousness. The 21st century all-seated version, though, is more economical with the grass verges, and the pitch-hugging stands make for a more compact arena.

As regards the cup-tie, it has to be said – and I am in no way biased – we totally outplayed Chelsea. In the second half especially, we peppered their goal, but a young 17-year-old goalkeeper called Steve Francis kept them in the match with a string of spectacular saves. It finished 0-0 and despite the prospect of a mouth-watering replay at Boothferry Park, I couldn't help feeling disappointed. We really should have won.

All that I had to do now was to negotiate my way around twenty thousand disgruntled Chelsea fans on my route back to the tube. The police guided us down an alleyway at the side of the stadium, which led onto a main road at the notorious Shed End. It appeared that most of the undesirable members of that stand were lying in wait for us. We were channelled along the road towards the waiting buses and the 'undesirables' kept us company on the opposite pavement, and they didn't look like happy bunnies. Despite having brains the size of peas, the Chelsea psychos were eventually able to deduce that the police presence was too great to risk kicking some Hull ass, and they gradually drifted away. I was able to make my break for the tube station, although I still half expected Mick to spring out and yell, "There he is! There's the Hull fan! Oh, and have I told you about his backward leap-frog?"

Thankfully, my passage home was a safe one. City lost the replay – Steve Francis again playing a blinder – and my chance to torment Mick had gone.

Funny the way things turn out: three years later, I ended up playing in the same Sunday League pub team as Mick – the 'Woodcock'. I was living in Barnet, and Mick's side were only a few miles up the road in Borehamwood, (or Elstree, as the posh people like to call it). Elstree, of course, is also home to the set of Eastenders, and on various occasions it was possible to spot members of the cast about town. One morning, I suffered a mild shock when I literally bumped into the intimidating 'Dirty Den' as he made his exit from a local newsagent. Then I remembered that Eastenders is just a fictional soap and I was able to relax and laugh at my foolish edginess. Then I remembered that Leslie Grantham had actually served time for killing someone, so I went into shock again.

A few years later, I began teaching in the area, and during one lunch break, I found myself behind the uncouth Ricky Butcher, (Sid Owen), in a sandwich bar. Despite not being in acting mode, Sid still proceeded to eat his sandwich like a pig. I wasn't aware initially of his chosen filling, but after watching it rotate around his mouth a few times like a tumble drier, I soon found out.

I played for Mick's pub team for seven seasons until I finally got fed up with the poor early morning turnouts. Most of the side required major assistance to be raised from their drink-induced comas, and we regularly had to kick off with less than the prescribed eleven. Sending-offs were also commonplace and we generally finished games with eight or nine men. I shall never forget one double sending off which must have spawned some unique explanations in the referee's report. We were 3-1 down in a semi-final, when the utterly incompetent ref awarded the opposition a highly dubious penalty. This was the final straw for Nicky, our right-sided midfielder, who launched a wet lump of mud in the ref's general direction, from way out on the touchline. To his sheer horror, the speculative throw turned out to be unbelievably accurate, and it caught the referee on the side of his face with a delicious smack. He wiped the mud from his eyes and looked around for the culprit. It wasn't hard to work it out. Nicky was whistling a happy tune and looking to the skies, but his red face and muddy right hand were a dead give away. He was immediately given his marching orders.

Meanwhile, Big Dave, our centre-back, who had missed the previous game after spending the night in police cells, found the whole situation hilarious. He was doubled over with laughter, pointing at the muddy-faced referee who was now looking like a highly flustered black and white minstrel. He sent Dave off for laughing at him. The ref stopped short, though, of bursting into tears, picking his ball up, and stomping off home. Just for the record, the penalty was eventually scored, and we lost 4-1.

We did have some successes too though, and we did make it to a few finals and these were normally played on a magnificent pitch in the grounds of Harperbury Hospital.

It was a fine surface on which to play a final, but there was one drawback: Harperbury was an institute for the mentally unstable, and most of the 'inmates' appeared to be given free rein to roam the grounds.

Vacant-looking intruders caused more than one stoppage in play; these were pitch invasions like no other. On one occasion, a happy couple strolled obliviously across the field of play brandishing a picnic hamper. It would have surprised no one if they had settled down in the centre circle to lay out a selection of sandwiches and cakes, but they kept on walking, gazing blankly ahead, as if enjoying a Sunday afternoon ramble in the park.

Another character appeared to be patrolling the area behind the goal, riding a tricycle that was several sizes too small for him. He seemed unable to take advantage of the extra stability that a three wheeled vehicle offers, and he regularly hit the deck. Balance and agility were obviously not his strong points, and this was further confirmed whenever the ball landed in his territory. His uncoordinated attempts to return it to the pitch would have tested the patience of the most saintly of saints, and it probably accounted for a fair percentage of the referee's stoppage time.

The players on the pitch were relatively safe, though, compared with those on the sidelines. Frank, our manager, told us afterwards of mysterious figures that kept sidling up to him, attempting to engage in conversations that belonged on a different planet. At one point, after feeling hot breath on his neck, he turned round to be confronted by a menacing looking chap of stocky build.

"THEY'VE CANCELLED THE WRESTLING!" he stated in a gruff tone.

Frank wasn't sure how to react. Was this news good or bad? Was the stranger on the lookout for someone to wrestle? Frank opted for the 'heart-felt commiserations approach', and the burly wrestler accordingly moved on to spread the bad news elsewhere.

In spite of all these distractions, I still won a nice collection of medals with the Woodcock, but a septic toenail prevented me from starting the 1993 campaign.

By November, it had healed and I elected to join a Saturday side in Hemel Hempstead, where standards were better and hangovers had usually been cleared by kick-off time. Mick soldiered on for another season with the Woodcock until they merged with a rival local side and his dodgy knees suggested that it was time to quit.

We still meet up on a regular basis. His three children are similar ages to my three, so get-togethers are usually over Sunday lunch, where we can discuss Chelsea and Hull City's rising fortunes; the wives can discuss shopping; and the six kids can run riot and play leap-frog around the house.

VENUE 17 – THE NEW DEN

Millwall 1 Hull City 1

Tuesday 14th February 2006 – 7.45pm

If you have a death wish, you might happily go hang-gliding, white-water rafting or swimming with sharks, but only a hopeless suicide case would deliberately walk into a lion's den.

Somehow, Mick has persuaded me to do just this by using his football contacts to procure freebie tickets in the Millwall end. Never one to look a gift-horse in the mouth, I have accepted the offering, fully aware that I will need to endure ninety minutes of faultless self-containment, or I'll be dead meat!

The tickets are coming via Neil Robinson – brother of Paul Robinson – Millwall's centre back. Neil plays for Hadley Wood, in the Herts Senior League – coached by Mick, and Paul used to be coached by Mick at school's district level. We are due to meet Neil outside the New Den at about 7.30pm to pick up the tickets, which sounds like a risky arrangement, but if plans go tits up, we can always pay our way into the City end, as it's not an all-ticket fixture.

At London Bridge Station, Mick and I meet up with Garv (another friend from our college days – and another witness of the infamous backward leapfrog). Garv supports AFC Wimbledon, and like most ex-Wimbledon fans, he refuses to acknowledge the MK Dons, so he now watches most of his football at non-league grounds. Tonight will be a rare treat for him.

After a short train journey to South Bermondsey, we make a right turn out of the station and start looking for a pub. As we walk, I practise my cockney accent on Mick and Garv. After years of watching Eastenders, I feel confident that I can carry it off. They disagree, and suggest that Dick Van Dyke would stand more chance of blending in with the local lions. Their advice is to shut up and let them do the talking. Suits me, it means that they'll have to get the beers in.

Just around the corner, we come across the Golden Lion, but it doesn't look very welcoming. The exterior could do with a serious lick of paint, and the thick iron bars on the windows hint towards a troubled past.

The interior is also desperately in need of refurbishment. Apart from the traditional bar in the centre, it has something of a youth club feel about it. A rather varied collection of chairs, sofas and tables are arranged around the edges of the room, looking suspiciously like charitable donations from local residents. Obviously, the landlord has made a conscious decision to avoid pointless investment in furniture due to the weekly carnage that precedes the football.

A further indication of impending violence is provided when our beers are served up in flimsy plastic beakers. At least we won't be getting glassed in the face tonight: well, not unless we leave through a window.

There's a fair smattering of Millwall tops around the place, so we find a nice quiet corner near the exit, ready for a quick getaway, but the call of nature soon necessitates a nervy walk to the opposite end of the bar. I make it safely to the urinal, but become unnerved by the imposing Millwall-shirted bruiser who loiters behind me next to the occupied cubicle. It crosses my mind that he may just be waiting here to duff up away fans, so I get prepared to use my Frank Butcher impression, but I'm saved by the flush of a chain. The cubicle door opens, and the bruiser darts inside, clearly desperate for a shit.

I make it back to our safe corner without any further alarms, but we still decide to move on while the going is good, and the search for food begins. The boys trust me to lead the way on this one, and within seconds, my Hull-grown instincts have guided us to a fine fish and chip establishment where I begin to eye up a few choice pieces of cod.

At the counter we bump into Neil Robinson, treating his girlfriend to an exotic Valentine's meal, but we learn that he is not yet in possession of the tickets. His Mum and Dad have got them, and they are still stuck in traffic. This does not overly worry me; in fact I'm secretly hoping that they won't show up, and I can drag Mick and Garv into the City end. They eventually make it, with about ten minutes to spare. Bugger!

Our seats are high up on the very back row of the West Stand. It is a great view, but as the game kicks off the stadium is disappointingly empty. Last week against Sheffield Wednesday, the attendance had topped 12 000, but this evening there can't be more than about 7 000 inside. Surely, the prospect of 'getting a leg over' on Valentine's evening has not accounted for the 5 000 absentees.

Paul Robinson's inclusion in Millwall's starting line up adds some extra spice to the contest, and my seat alongside the whole of his family makes me especially mindful of my anti-Millwall responses to the match action.

In the early stages, he looks quite solid in the air, but suspect to Fagan's pace on the deck. Worried by the latter, he slices a back pass out for a City corner, and the entire West Stand call for him to be strung up. The Robinsons all sink a little lower into their seats.

Worse is to come when Fagan breaks away and exposes a lack of pace in the whole back four, but their blushes are spared by the Lions' keeper, Andy Marshall, who races from his line to put the City striker off. The ball wastefully runs out for a goal kick.

City are now taking control, and another lively run from Fagan sets up Parkin for a twelve yard strike, but the big man pulls it wide. The City fans away to my left, high up behind the far goal, immediately echo:

"Feed the Beast and he will score…" which seems a bit wide of the mark: he just missed, didn't he?

With half time approaching, Fagan again gets the alarm bells ringing in the Millwall defence as Andrews' long ball puts Robinson in a pickle. Again Fagan is clean through, and again Marshall comes steaming out like an express train to faze him, but Robinson is taking no chances. He stretches out his leg and trips Fagan as he is about to round the keeper. This conveniently helps Fagan to fall out of harms way, avoiding the high-speed collision between Marshall and the unfortunate Robinson, who consequently hits the deck like a sack of spuds, unconscious. The medics are immediately called for.

I'm really pleased with myself for managing to curb my initial instinct to stand up and yell, "Send the dirty bastard off!"

The referee is not so restrained. He brandishes a red card as the stretcher-bearers cart the dazed Robinson away.

Elliott lines up the free kick, and I worry that if he scores, things might turn a bit nasty. I can hardly expect the shell-shocked Robinsons to offer protection to the Hull City git who sits amongst them. Elliott's kick curls wide, and I'm strangely relieved, but eleven Tigers will surely overcome ten ineffective Lions in the second half.

Mr and Mrs Robinson disappear during the interval to check on the damage to their son. They return in time for the second half with the news that he is now fully conscious, and keen to get back on the pitch. Sure Paul: after your three match ban!

Millwall compensate for Robinson's loss by coming out with just three in midfield. City sort of take advantage of this by dominating possession, but despite the numerical advantage, we continually fail to make the final killer pass.

The Tigers back four have also had to reorganise. Collins has picked up a knee injury, and Alton Thelwell has come on at left back, allowing Delaney to move into the middle. Mick notices this, so I launch into a lengthy explanation about Thelwell's recent comeback, and Delaney's preferred position in the centre. I'm sounding far too knowledgeable, and I'm talking far too loud. Mick thanks me for the information and tells me to shut up.

It's beginning to look like a 0-0 draw until Andrews finally splits the Millwall defence with an accurate ball into Parkin's path. The Beast takes one touch with his right foot, then one touch with his left, and the ball is nestling in the back of the net.

I stifle my celebration admirably, like in Tom and Jerry when Tom sits on a pin. Two Hull infiltrators close by are not quite so controlled, and within a minute, they have been frog-marched out by stewards. Apparently, they use CCTV cameras to keep a close watch on the crowd and I begin to wonder if I might be the next person with an invitation to 'come on down.' The stewards are clearly getting more messages through their earpieces and they seem to be gesturing in my general direction.

Just as I think that my days are numbered, Millwall score, and I muster quite a convincing celebratory reaction, which does just enough to defuse their suspicion. I stand applauding, but inwardly, I am seething. We barely managed to hang onto the lead for two minutes, and it was another shot from outside the box. That's 9 out of 25 goals in away games that have flown in from range. It's getting silly.

The last ten minutes are a little tense as Millwall finish the stronger. Ryan France is given a torrid time by substitute, Marvin Williams, but honours end even.

My phone goes off as we shuffle out of the ground. It's my brother,

Mike, in Madrid. A rather monosyllabic match report follows, as I'm surrounded by the enemy. I don't want to come out with any give away lines like:

"Millwall are a bunch of fairies. We should have mullered them!"

This policy is maintained on the packed train until we get off at Edgware with three other City fans. They have got a four-hour drive ahead of them, which won't get them home until about 3am, and they all have to be at work at nine. This makes me feel a bit better. There is no way I could have completed this season-long challenge if I still lived in Hull.

COMPANION 18

Name: **Peter Collingwood**
Birthplace: **Hull**
Relationship: **Brother**
Allegiance: **Hull City**

Relevant History

I can vividly remember the day that my little baby brother was first brought into the house and placed on my lap. I remember the first time that he crawled, the first time that he walked, and the first time that he swam.

I've been there for his football firsts too. Peter may have tried to forget, but I can still clearly remember that his first football kit was a Chelsea one, with a number five on the back for one of the ugliest players in the football league - Micky Droy – a thick set centre half with long hair, scraggy beard and a flat nose.

Thankfully, sanity prevailed for his first visit to a football ground. It was April 1975, and Blackpool were the visitors to Boothferry Park. The Tigers won it 1-0 with a late John Hawley header, and the Withernsea born striker instantly became Peter's new hero. He was the local boy made good, with a knack for scoring spectacular goals, the most memorable of which, had come earlier that season in a 3-1 win against Sunderland. It was a shot of great ferocity into the top corner, which left Jim Montgomery grasping at thin air.

The goal made such an impression on Peter, that he was inspired to write to Fred Dineage on Yorkshire TV's Big Match pleading for a re-screening in the Golden Goals feature. Mass hysteria ensued in the Collingwood household a few weeks later when Fred looked us all in the eye and read out Peter's name. We were so busy leaping about and jumping on Peter that we missed the re-run.

Despite possessing a venomous and accurate shot, Hawley always used to claim that his career ambition was to launch a direct hit at the North Stand clock. He was never able to achieve it, but some of his clueless colleagues did, although they were trying to achieve their career ambition of scoring a goal.

Hawley moved on to seek his fortune at Elland Road, which coincidentally, is where Peter watched his first away fixture. Leeds United's home ground was chosen as the neutral venue for City's second replay against Blyth Spartans in the 3rd round of the FA Cup in 1980.

Again, I was there to witness another of Peter's football firsts, although we didn't travel together. He went by car with a friend, while I chose the more reliable option of the Football Express from Paragon Station. Bad decision. It broke down en route, and we didn't get there until half time.

Still, it was a memorable match for Peter's first away trip, and I didn't lose out in the end either, as it went to extra time and Stuart Croft won it with a late header.

Since then, we have been to many away matches together, but the most memorable would have to be the 2003 encounter at Northampton, one of those days when everything went right.

On the previous Tuesday, City had gone top of League Division Three with a 1-0 home win over Swansea in front of a full house at the KC Stadium. Songs about our new 'top of the league' status featured heavily therefore, in the pre-match build up, and they bore increasing relevance as we swept into a 2-0 half time lead.

The fifteen-minute interval provided further priceless entertainment. A Northampton fan was challenged to hit the woodwork with shots from the edge of the area. If he could succeed on two of the three attempts, he would become the proud owner of a brand new Toyota car. He failed miserably, but then the real fun began, when a Hull City fan was hauled from the crowd to try his luck.

Initially, we offered a rousing cheer and gave him our full backing in the hope that he could defy the odds – then we realised that the guy was absolutely arseholed, and was more likely to hit the corner flags; that's if his double vision could work out which of the two footballs to kick.

In his fuddled state, he appeared not even to understand the object of the exercise. He slammed his first effort into the centre of the goal, and set off in true celebratory style with his replica City shirt pulled up over his head. It was quite a task for the MC to coax him back for a second attempt, and it reminded me very much of some of my teaching experiences where I have had to humour an awkward and temperamental child whilst trying desperately not to lose my cool.

The second and third attempts were equally wayward, and there was an audible sigh of relief from all around the ground that this drunken maniac would not be let loose on the streets of Northampton tonight behind the wheel of a new car.

The players were eventually able to get back on the pitch, and the goals continued to flow. The third was an absolute cracker, and convinced us that promotion was going to be a formality. Price released Allsopp down the right, and then he charged into the area to get on the end of the cross, flinging himself at the ball to head home. Price's momentum carried him into the back of the net, where he stayed to celebrate with the fans.

Steve Harper, the Northampton keeper and nephew of a dinner lady at my school, then got himself sent off for pulling down Allsopp. It was looking bleak for the Cobblers, but fortunes briefly rallied when the replacement keeper saved the penalty, and then Paul Trollope pulled a goal back.

End of brief rally: Burgess made it 4-1, and then with a cruel twist of the knife, former Northampton player, Jamie Forrester, made it five. Cue mass exodus of Northampton fans. They were all clearly visible on a large embankment behind the petite West Stand and they weren't going to get away with an early exit.

"We can see you sneaking out..."

"Can you hear us on the hill..." to name but two of the songs aimed in their direction.

It was a great occasion. Having suffered too many false dawns in the previous seasons, the sun was finally shining on the Tigers, and as Peter and I headed back down the M1, we were in complete agreement about one thing:

"We must do this more often."

VENUE 18 – NINIAN PARK

Cardiff City 1 Hull City 0

Saturday 18th February 2006 – 3pm

An interesting payment system exists at the Severn Bridge. It costs £4.50 to get into Wales, but it is free to leave. I can't help thinking that they've missed out on a major money making opportunity here. Surely, people would pay anything to get out of Wales.

Once on the other side, we are guided to the ground by brightly lit signs (coincidentally, with amber writing on a black background) advising all Hull City fans to exit at Junction 33. As a result, we arrive nice and early, but drive straight past Ninian Park in search of pubs. There are a couple of possibilities on the other side of the road so we turn round in an entrance to Cardiff Arms Park, and double-back to the West Gate.

At first glance, this pub seems more geared towards the rugby fraternity. Several flags of the Welsh dragon hang outside, and a variety of match action photos from the Arms Park adorn the walls inside. Many of the drinkers are wearing the red jersey of the national Rugby Union side, and not one Cardiff City top is evident. It's as if we've got our dates mixed up, and we've arrived on a Six Nations day. It's a worrying thought.

Despite the obvious leaning towards an inferior game, all the TV screens are still showing the 5th round FA Cup tie between Liverpool and Man United, so we settle down for a quick pint. It's a good old-fashioned blood and thunder tie, but we only stay until half time. Our priority is to get parked near the ground, so we forego the pub lunch. The mega full English cooked breakfast that Peter's wife, Christina, prepared for us at nine o'clock this morning will have to see us through.

Parking is easy, thanks to the large car park that sits between Ninian Park and the Leckwith Athletics Stadium. It may all look very different if I revisit in the future, though, as the Leckwith track is the proposed site for Cardiff City's dream new stadium. Plans are still a couple of years from fruition, but as Peter and I enter the Grange End of their present home, it becomes clear that the move cannot come soon enough. Ninian Park is a tired old place, and I wonder what they will do in the interim if they somehow manage to scrape into the Premiership.

The capacity here is 20 000, but a fair proportion of this is old-fashioned terracing, where it's standing room only. The only other ground where I've encountered this in the Championship is at Plymouth.

The Tigers fans are positioned to the left of the goal. Most are standing, but five hundred seats have been tucked away in the bottom corner. Peter and I have got tickets for this section, but it's a relief to learn that we are allowed to sit anywhere. Our ticket numbers of F6 and F7 would have placed us at the very far end, with a quarter of the pitch obscured by the Grandstand. Actually, the Grandstand is anything but grand, although I'm sure it was impressive in 1920.

Opposite this, we have the Popular Bank. Popular as opposed to what, I wonder? The lower tier of this consists of another large section of terracing, as does the other half of the Grange End, where the rowdiest Cardiff fans are already in fine voice. The City fans are unusually quiet, and then I realise why.

Standing just near me, finishing off a pre-match beer, is the relentless 'Lead Singer.' I tell Peter about the man's impressive capacity to sing non-stop throughout the entire match, and about how I got stuck behind him at Wolves and Leeds. The vehement vocalist crumples up a plastic beer container with his bare hand and brushes us aside, before disappearing into the crowd of City fans that are waiting patiently on the terrace. Within three seconds, everyone bursts into song. The choirmaster has arrived.

As the game kicks off, hundreds of fans are still arriving over the brow of the far corner terrace. They are overlooked by a towering floodlight pylon, and it reminds me a little of how the latecomers used to file into the north eastern corner of Boothferry Park. Much as I love the KC Stadium, I do still get the odd nostalgic pang for our former home, and it's the old grounds like Ninian Park and Kenilworth Road that send me down Memory Lane.

Honours are even on the pitch in the first ten minutes. Cameron Jerome is clearly the main threat, and I pray that our two full backs do not get tested for pace. Thelwell is making his first start for over a year, and it's been a while for Alan Rogers too.

The atmosphere is terrific. For the first time this season, the travelling City fans are facing real competition in the singing stakes. The absence of seats in the Grange End Stand has allowed a large ensemble of willing Cardiff singers to congregate on the other side of the narrow segregation area, and as we know, all Welsh people think they can sing. The favourite song of the City fans today is:

"Sheep-shaggers, sheep-shaggers."

I am pleased to see that Cardiff are not testing out our full-backs, as they repeatedly pump long balls through for Jerome, but unfortunately, this tactic actually works. On seventeen minutes another long punt sees Delaney and Myhill get in a right muddle, allowing the lively nineteen year-old striker to lob the ball into an empty net. The Cardiff fans love this.

"One-nil, to the sheep-shaggers…" they sing.

The sheep-shaggers are on top, but City are not going to take it lying down, if you pardon the innuendo. A dogged run by Parkin releases Rogers down the left, and his cross evades everyone except Parkin who appears late at the far post. He unleashes a thunderous shot, which is somehow blocked on the line, or was it over the line? Parkin certainly seems to think so, and he stands with his arms outstretched appealing to the linesman. It may even have been hand-ball: it happened so quickly it's hard to tell.

It further strengthens my belief that goal line technology should be in use at all football league games. There is nothing more frustrating for a striker, than to have a perfectly good goal ruled out by sleepy officials. I should know. I'm still bitter about a Sunday League effort of mine from 1987 which must have crept at least a foot over the line. The original referee hadn't turned up, so the manager of the opposing team was 'impartially' filling the breach. He coached them as a hobby, even though he had just been signed by Wimbledon from non-league Wealdstone. His name? Vinnie Jones. Funnily enough, no one argued with his decision.

MicroGen was the name of Vinnie's side, but I'm not sure what that stood for. Possibly, it was an abbreviation of Microscopic Genitals, which would explode the myth that he's got 'two smoking barrels.'

Anyway, Parkin's appeals fall on deaf ears, and Cardiff hang on to their slender lead.

Ellison is also short of luck as he sees his precise goal-bound curling shot expertly turned round the post by the sprawling Neil Alexander.

Half time arrives, and we join the queue for refreshments at a wonky old hut. Here, I witness a wonderful example of the language barrier between East Yorkshire and South Wales, even though we all technically speak English. The gangly teenager in front of me is having trouble placing his simple order.

"A kirk please," he requests politely.

"Pardon?"

"A kirk please," he patiently repeats.

"A what?"

"A kirka curler."

"Oh, a coke."

"Yeah, that's what I said!!"

Benny Hill couldn't have scripted it any better.

We sup our coffees whilst watching an ill-conceived competition, where contenders attempt to score from the halfway line. The whole thing looks like a bit of a 'spur of the moment' idea, as they all seem to be dressed in smart clothes and shoes. As a result, no one even comes close, and the participating Tigers fan causes us acute embarrassment by scuffing his effort in the direction of the corner flag before it runs out of puff on the corner of the penalty box. It is a merciful release when the players reappear from the tunnel to resume the action.

The unrelenting singing rivalry continues throughout the second half, punctuated only by the occasional sheep impression. Another faction of Welsh singers have positioned themselves in the corner of the Grandstand, so we're getting it from both sides.

Peter and I have moved out of the seats for the second half, believing that it may be our last ever opportunity to stand at a football match - without being told off by a steward. Standing in front of us is an elderly gentleman who is becoming thoroughly wound up by taunts from the Grandstand. Somehow, he has made eye contact with one particular Cardiff fan, and they engage in a heated argument, even though they are at least fifty metres apart. Our irate pensioner friend makes it clear that he will meet his Welsh counterpart outside after the game for a bout of good old-fashioned fisty-cuffs. This causes great merriment in the Grandstand, where the rival fan mimes a great big belly laugh.

They eventually return their focus towards the game, where the Tigers are very much on top. Cardiff's only threat comes from a couple of Koumas free kicks. City then look like they are going to get back in it when Parkin is ruthlessly taken out when clean through on goal. It might be a red card offence, and it may even be a penalty. The ref gives neither. It's a free kick on the edge, and it's not even a booking.

With ten minutes remaining, it becomes obvious that Cardiff are settling for 1-0 when they take off the dangerous Jerome and replace him with an extra defender. City take full advantage and pepper the Cardiff goal. Green has a shot blocked on the line, there are countless scrambles, and Alexander is called into action more than once.

We enter stoppage time, and an aerial midfield challenge on the halfway line causes the ball to loop out for a City throw. It drops straight to Dave Jones, the Cardiff manager, but instead of neatly trapping it, he nonchalantly flicks it away towards the corner flag, wasting another valuable twenty seconds. Normally, a blatant act of time wasting such as this would warrant a booking, but today of course, the referee has left his cards at home.

Elliott very nearly nicks a point in the last minute, but Alexander again saves well. The final whistle sounds, and the aggressive pensioner in front of us immediately marches purposefully towards the exit. He's either ready for a fight, or he's making a run for it. There is no sign of trouble when we get outside, so we assume that it's the latter.

It has been a disappointing defeat, but Cardiff are competing for a play off place, and we've just out played them. It just goes to show that there is a fine line between success and failure in this division.

Peter and I waste no time in heading back towards the Severn Bridge. We pray that it is still free to get out of Wales.

COMPANION 19

Name: Kevin Clancy
Birthplace: Hampstead, London
Relationship: Brother-in-law
Allegiance: Chelsea

Relevant History

Kevin is a bit of a Chelsea anorak. He's a season ticket holder, his house is full of Chelsea memorabilia, and he even bothers to phone in to Chelsea Radio to make his views known to all - as if anyone cares.

His obsession goes completely unchecked by his wife, Maura; she is a season ticket holder too, and if anything, she is even more fanatical than Kevin. Not much can prevent her from missing a home game, except maybe a Christmas shopping trip to New York, which is how I came to take a seat next to Kevin for the 2003 encounter with Manchester United. She couldn't have picked a better weekend for a bit of trans-Atlantic retail therapy.

In order to accommodate the TV cameras, the kick off had been shifted to four o'clock on a Sunday afternoon, ideal for a pre-match lunch and a few beers. From Fulham Broadway, we headed straight for the Blue Spice Curry House, where we met up with Kevin's brother-in-law, John, his friend Bruce (not an Australian) and Bruce's two teenage sons.

I was soon joining in with their traditional practice of betting on Claudio Ranieri's starting line-up. Coins were slapped into the middle of the table as we embarked on the impossible task of predicting the outcome of the Tinkerman's revolving-door squad rotation system. No one had even come close so far this season and the kitty had built up to quite a substantial amount.

We all agreed that John Terry and Frank Lampard were certain starters, but after that, it was anyone's guess. We all turned out to be hopelessly wrong, and none of us foresaw the strike force pairing of Mutu and Crespo.

The curry warmed us up nicely for a cold afternoon in the upper tier of the West Stand, and a fervent pre-match vocal contest between the two sets of fans warmed us up even more. As the players waited nervously in the tunnel, the big screen projected live pictures of a giant John Terry, looking down on his dominions, like some kind of demigod.

I have to admit; the God-like status of top players has diminished in my eyes over the years, as most of them are now half my age, and I'm peeved that they rake in 150 times my salary for doing something they love. I worked out recently that it would take me three years to earn what Rio Ferdinand earns in a week, and I'm a fully qualified teacher with twenty years experience. I think, rather than awe and wonder, it tends to be feelings of jealousy and injustice nowadays.

It irritated me even more to think that Rio was about to begin a fully paid eight-month sabbatical from the game, thanks to his inability to remember a simple drugs test. Well, they do say that a footballer loses thousands of brain cells every time he heads a football, so I suppose he had an excuse.

Anyway, Terry was finally allowed to lead his troops out onto the pitch to the strains of Suggs' 1997 offering – Blue Day. Stamford Bridge is surely the only place where his No. 22 smash still receives airplay.

After the vibrant build up, the match itself was a bit of a letdown. Defences dominated, Ruud van Nistelrooy hardly got a look in, and the game was settled by a Frank Lampard penalty.

Still, Kevin seemed happy, and he dragged me into the Chelsea Village afterwards to celebrate, adding a few more pence to the Abramovich coffers.

It was about 7.30pm by the time we emerged and headed back towards the tube. Just as we passed the Stamford Bridge gates, a posh car swung out and joined the snail's pace traffic. Sitting in the passenger seat was Claudio Ranieri. Immediately, swarms of fans buzzed around the vehicle, flashing their camera phones through the tinted glass window, Kevin included. Goodness me, you'd think he was some kind of God.

Actually, despite only achieving modest success with the Russian billions, he was held in high esteem by the Chelsea faithful, and they had become particularly protective of him since Abramovich was snapped colluding with Sven.

The mood changed later in the season when the Tinkerman's tactical substitutions in Monaco completely blew their chance of making it into the Champions League Final.

The traffic finally got moving, and Claudio was given a bit of peace, although a few persistent fans continued to chase the car over the horizon. Kevin and I continued the walk to the station.

It had been an enjoyable Premiership experience, despite the lack of goalmouth action. I thanked Kevin for the invite, but reminded him that he owed me one, and would now be expected to accompany me to a Tigers match in the very near future.

VENUE 19 – THE WALKERS STADIUM

Leicester City 3 Hull City 2

Saturday 4th March 2006 – 3pm

The area around the Walkers Stadium seems to be devoid of drinking establishments, but after a prolonged search and a few discreet enquiries, we finally come across the perfect family pub, and happily for Kevin, it is screening the one o'clock clash between West Brom and Chelsea.

We are undeterred by the sign in the doorway, which firmly decrees that no away supporters are allowed. Clearly, many other Tigers fans have also ignored the warning, and it is easy to pick them out as we wriggle through to the bar. They are the ones without Leicester City shirts on.

A vacant table is found, and we settle down to enjoy our beer and burgers, but a lady with a clipboard soon interrupts our peace. It is half time in the Chelsea match, so Kevin agrees to help out with a market research questionnaire. Her initial enquiries appear harmless, but I grow a little suspicious as the questions become increasingly loaded.

"How far have you travelled today?"

"How often do you come here?"

"What is your address?"

This is surely a ploy to weed out the away supporters, and I'm waiting for her to deliver the final killer question in a loud accusing Gestapo tone, for the entire pub to hear:

"And for how long have you been supporting HULL CITY, YOU NORTHERN SVINE!!!??"

I refuse to play ball, and the 'no comment' strategy is applied. Actually, as Kevin lives in Wembley, he has not had to be too evasive, and it is only the question about his age that has caused him concern. Our interrogator had to use her most persuasive techniques to prise that one out of him, although she stopped short of the thumbscrews.

By 2.30pm we have moved on to the stadium, but alarmingly long queues are tracing away from the City turnstiles. Incredibly, only two turnstiles have been opened to filter our 3 000 travelling fans. Kevin and I join the end of one of the lengthy lines, and in the first five minutes, we move about five inches. The police are taking all the flak, but they are at pains to point out that it is not their fault, and that there is an acute shortage of stewards at the ground.

The tension is slightly defused by some humorous songs: "Shit ground, no staff..." but as three o'clock draws nearer, and the likelihood of missing the first half due to gross incompetence increases, the anxiety returns and a Kaiser Chiefs song is adopted: "I predict a riot, I predict a riot..."

Finally, an extra turnstile is opened up, and they wisely decide to accept a round twenty quid instead of an awkward twenty-three. We stream through quickly, and only miss the first five minutes.

The design of the ground is startlingly similar to that of the St. Mary's Stadium in Southampton, and the feeling of déjà vu is intensified by our placement in the North Stand, where the blinding sun shines directly into our eyes, just as it did on the south coast last October. Despite all this, it's hard to forget where we are. Hundreds of Walkers Crisps emblems decorate the front edge of the roof, and giant Gary Lineker banners overlook the outer turnstiles. As if this is not enough, I then flick through the programme and allow more Walkers adverts to probe my sub conscious.

I manage to turn my thoughts away from crisps, and towards the game. Leicester appear content to hoof long balls through the middle, but most are over hit, and they just roll through to Boaz. Then, with their first decent attack, the Foxes take the lead.

Joey Gudjonsson releases Iain Hume (surely, a mile offside) and he curls a perfect shot into the bottom corner of the net with the outside of his right boot. He peels away for a half-hearted celebration, half expecting it to be curtailed by the linesman's flag, but he gets away with it.

The lead is short-lived though. Stuart Green feeds the Beast; the Beast feeds an unmarked Stuart Elliott, and he heads home to level the scores. It's a well-worked goal, and it's fully deserved.

Knowing how Kevin loves questionnaires, I use the half time break to conduct a little market research of my own. He is a season ticket holder at Stamford Bridge and I am interested to know how Championship football compares with the Premiership.

Apparently, 'movement off the ball' is the big difference – in the Championship, there isn't any. Consequently, options are limited for the man on the ball; composure is uncommon, and possession is short-lived.

Midway through the second half, Leicester regain the lead with a bolt from the blue, literally. There appears to be no danger as Gudjohhnson takes up possession on the half way line, but he spots Myhill off his line and applies the perfect trajectory to his lofted drive, causing our stranded keeper to do a brilliant David Seaman impression.

Admittedly, it's a great piece of opportunism, and the home crowd go crazy, no doubt spilling lots of crisps in the process. It also serves to crank up the singing, and they take great pleasure in trying to put us in our place with a chant that is short and to the point:

"Sit down, shut up.

"Sit down, shut up!"

Their put-downs appear to backfire however, as City fight back to enjoy their best spell of the game. Parkin sees a point-blank effort brilliantly tipped over by Paul Henderson, and then Green volleys narrowly wide. It's beginning to look like it's not going to be our day, when a great piece of control and skill from Parkin sets up a low strike from Green. It finds the corner of the net, and suddenly all 3 000 City fans break into a few immensely satisfying verses of, "Sit down, shut up..." They do as they're told.

It's still anybody's game, but the closer we get to full time, the deeper the Tigers defend, and the more trouble they have clearing their lines. The inevitable happens with just five minutes left. The ball is played square to the dangerous Gudjonsson on the edge of the box, and he fully utilises the time and space on offer, before striking yet another long distance shot into Myhill's net.

In the final minutes, we are unable to seriously trouble Henderson, although Myhill does his best to seriously trouble himself. Having wandered up to the half way line to lend his support to the attack, he completely skies a clearance, but instead of racing back to his goal, he stays upfield and tries to put in a challenge. A midfield general he is not, and Leicester's Andy Welsh dribbles past him, and all the way to the edge of the box, where he finally decides it is safe to shy at the empty net. Incredibly, he puts it over. It's the last action of the match, and we have now gained a measly two points out of the last fifteen. It is very frustrating, because we've been playing well without picking up the points. It's another reminder that you can't take anything for granted in this division.

As we leave the Walkers Stadium and pass the Gary Lineker banner for the final time, I get a sudden inexplicable urge for a packet of cheese and onion crisps.

COMPANION 20

Name: Elizabeth Collingwood
Birthplace: Hemel Hempstead
Relationship: Daughter
Allegiance: England

Relevant History

Like all proud fathers, I had longed for the day when I could take my first-born child along to her first football match. It can be a life-shaping experience, and a whole host of factors have to be considered: the weather, the ground, the company, the opposition, the team news - in fact, the whole day needs to be intricately planned to guarantee that the young victim begs for more of the same, and inherits the same blind allegiance towards your favourite team.

I was carefully biding my time with Lizzie. She was very involved in sport at school, and had shown a promising level of interest in England's fixtures at the 2002 World Cup. Hull City were poised to move into a brand new stadium, so I had pencilled her in for an Easter debut at the KC, when she would be ten years old, the weather would be warmer, and City would hopefully be sitting at the top of Division Three.

Imagine my horror, therefore, when without warning; her friend's Dad snatched the whole experience away from me. September 21st 2002 was the exact date. It had started off as a normal Saturday: I had flown round the supermarket to do the weekly shop, rushed out to play football for my Saturday side, and dropped Lizzie off at her friend's house to play.

The afternoon went well too. We won our match 2-1 and I enjoyed a couple of relaxing post-match shandies in the White Swan at Garston. Even Jan Molby's struggling Tigers did their bit by securing a goalless draw away at Oxford.

But, at 5.30, as I wearily turned the key in my front door, I was greeted by an excitable Lizzie who came bounding down the hallway. Thinking that I would be pleased, she broke the news that she had spent the day at Vicarage Road watching a six-goal thriller between Watford and Crystal Palace. The Hornets had been 3-2 down at half time but had fought back to secure a 3-3 draw.

I had to admit that it certainly sounded like an exciting match, but I wasn't sure if this was good or bad. Maybe, a boring 0-0 draw would have been more beneficial, creating a yearning to witness a more entertaining brand of football at the KC Stadium next spring; or would a goalless 90 minutes have put her off football for good?

I decided to let things lie for a while. She needed to realise that all games do not produce six goals, and she also needed to be locked up on Saturday afternoons. I couldn't risk a repeat occurrence of the Watford visit or it could become a regular event, and she would then try to drag me into it. Football can be an expensive pastime, and it's extremely galling if you don't even support the team before you.

Three years on, she is ready for the full Hull City match-day treatment: an early start, a pub meal, a fervent crowd in a decent stadium, and the right result. I asked her recently if she could remember the score of the 2002 meeting between Watford and Crystal Palace: she couldn't. Excellent news!

VENUE 20 – PORTMAN ROAD

Ipswich Town 1 Hull City 1

Saturday 25th April 2006 – 3pm

'WELCOME TO CHELMSFORD - COUNTY TOWN OF ESSEX, AND THE BIRTHPLACE OF RADIO.'

This is the proud boast, posted across the informative sign at Chelmsford's outer limits. Our knowledge of telecommunications history is sketchy, to say the least, so we are a little confused by the extravagant claim, and it is not until we reach Leo's house that we become enlightened.

Leo is a friend of a friend, a lifelong Ipswich fan and a Chelmsford resident, so he is able to explain the radio connection. Apparently, it was from Chelmsford that Marconi made his first regular radio broadcasts. Well, actually, it was from a hut in a village outside Chelmsford, so the town's claim to fame is not strictly true, but their only other claim to fame is that the 1970's sit-com 'Porridge' was filmed in Chelmsford prison. They're hardly likely to advertise this at the City gates.

'WELCOME TO CHELMSFORD – THE BIRTHPLACE OF PORRIDGE.'

Such a statement would be even more confusing, and could lead to some angry counter-claims from visiting Scots.

Anyway, enough about Chelmsford; Ipswich is our destination, and Leo insists that he can squeeze Lizzie and me into his people carrier for the remaining forty miles. His family of five are all season ticket holders, but his eldest daughter (seventeen-year-old Rebecca) is allegedly staying at home to focus on her 'A' level revision, and Leo believes this. It sounds like she's lost the faith to me.

The A12 is reasonably clear, although we are nearly forced to double-back when Leo realises that he's forgotten his lucky scarf. I manage to persuade him that such superstitions are just a load of old baloney, and anyway, there will be thousands of other Ipswich fans in the ground, equally convinced that their lucky scarves, hats and pants can influence the outcome of the match.

We find a space in the station car park and begin the walk into town. The rest of Leo's family are thoroughly decked out in blue and white, more than making up for the neglected scarf, and I worry that my fraternization with the enemy could lead to an ironic kicking from City fans, but there is not much sign of black and amber inside our chosen pub, Lloyds Tavern.

Leo, Bernadette, Joseph (15) and Dominique (13) are match-day regulars here and they recommend it highly. The food is unbelievably cheap, but it also takes an unbelievably long time to arrive. Forty-five minutes after placing my fish and chips order, I'm still waiting, and I suspect that they may have sneaked out to the nearby River Orwell with a fishing rod.

Fortunately, a vacant pool table helps to pass the time, and Joseph challenges the girls to a frame or two. Hustler Joe is clearly a seasoned veteran, and he instantly sets about his business, until Lizzie somehow puts together an impressive run of fluke trick shots, or as she puts it, "I keep accidentally scoring goals!"

It's a classic example of beginners luck, and it reminds me of the Two Ronnies sketch, where Barker beats Corbett at 'squish.' Her luck soon runs out though, and Joseph regains his credibility, although I find it hard to take him seriously when he's got 'Tractorboys' emblazoned across his back. It sounds like a jibe that the opposition would invent to take the piss, and as self-depreciating nicknames go, it can only be bettered by Cardiff's 'Sheepshaggers.'

Lunch eventually arrives, and as we chew the food, we also chew over our match predictions. Bernadette and Leo go for a 2-1 Ipswich win; Joseph and Dominique (both still young and wildly optimistic) go for a high scoring Ipswich rout, while Lizzie sits on the fence with a 1-1 draw – exactly what I was going to say. If I were in any way superstitious, I would consider it an omen.

Leo, of course, is hopelessly superstitious, and he is now banging on about how Ipswich always win when it's sunny. He is peering out of the window at the clear blue sky, jubilant that his lucky scarf wasn't needed after all. A sentence comes to mind, which includes the words 'straws' and 'clutching.'

We forego pudding, and make the short walk to Portman Road, where we part company at a statue of Bobby Robson. An agreement is made to meet at the same spot after the game, but of course, there is a risk that this may not happen if Hull City give them a good thrashing.

Lizzie and I follow Bobby Robson's pointing finger and locate the away turnstiles, but my innocent daughter must look like trouble in the eyes of the law, for they instantly search her dainty little handbag. Thankfully, she has left the carving knife on the kitchen table.

They allow her to pass, and we find our seats, which are at the very back of the Cobbold Stand amongst the rowdy element. A number of policemen and stewards immediately gather in the aisle right next to Lizzie. They really don't trust her.

Their presence turns out to be counter-productive. Whenever the Tigers attack the far goal, our minders obscure the view, so we have to stand. They then insist that we all sit down or we'll be ejected, but if they would just sod off, we wouldn't need to stand at all. It's Catch 22.

Just when they get us nicely seated, it's guaranteed that some wise guy will sing, "Stand up if you're Hull City..." and the whole rigmarole begins again. One fan to our left is becoming particularly incensed, and he enters into a tit-for-tat argument. A policeman gives him several warnings to shut up and sit down, but he just doesn't know when to quit and he succeeds in getting himself thrown out after barely ten minutes play.

Thirteen minutes later, Ipswich are awarded a free kick on the touchline beneath us.

Darren Currie takes it and curls a dangerous inswinger into the box. Nobody makes contact, but the ball continues on its curved route and finds its way into the far corner of the net. It's an absolute fluke, and it's obvious that there can only be one explanation for the freak effort: an over abundance of lucky scarves.

After half an hour I'm desperate for the loo, so I leave Lizzie alone with the rowdy rabble. When I return I ask her for a progress report. Apparently, there has been no goalmouth action, but Ian Westlake went down as if pole-axed, and the singing City faithful intimated that he should receive an Oscar.

There is a recurring theme for most of the Tigers' songs today. There is very little noise coming from the home fans, so the lyrics tend to relate to the deathly hush:

"One nil up – you still won't sing…"

"Just like a library…"

"Sit down and read a book…"

"No noise, from the Tractorboys…"

"Shhh, shhhh…"

None of these fine efforts are successful in coaxing a response, but finally, a loud-mouthed genius comes up with a solution. In the middle of the City end he begins to chant, "COME ON IPSWICH, COME ON IPSWICH…"

The entire City following joins in, and eventually, a faint echo emanates from the South Stand, triggering a congratulatory return cheer.

At the break, we take a stroll down to the cramped bar area, but immediately make a u-turn as the tiny space is struggling to accommodate all of the refreshment seekers and toilet goers. I'm relieved that I relieved myself earlier.

Instead, we watch the novel half time entertainment, which centres on a small group of groundsmen, who adopt a random formation, before stabbing the turf with large pitchforks. The time just flies by, and the players are soon appearing for the second half.

It is a fairly tame resumption, and chances are few and far between, but on 57 minutes we force a corner. Green and Ellison decide to take it short, and I berate them from on high, frustrated that they have wasted a golden opportunity to swing the ball into the box. But then, just to prove that I know sod all, Greeny floats in a dream cross which Leon Cort dispatches with a clinical nod of the head. The Tigers are level, and the sun has gone in, which is great news. According to the 'Law of Leo,' Ipswich cannot now win.

The final twenty minutes are really quite entertaining. Ipswich hit the post and bar, and Ellison sets off on a couple of trademark surging runs to create two great chances for the Tigers. The second of these produces a cross, which appears to be landing on a plate for Parkin at the back post, but Scott Barron somehow scrambles it clear.

Lizzie jumps off her seat, ready to celebrate the goal. She really seems to be getting involved. She even carries out the instinctive 'hands on head' routine that every football fan exercises following a near miss. Most encouraging.

It ends 1-1. Our prediction was correct, and when we meet up again with Leo, I remind him of that £50 wager we had. Well, it was worth a try.

On the road back to Chelmsford, we tune into BBC Radio Suffolk, and their early evening phone-in is exploring the reasons for the eerie silence on the Portman Road terraces. Exasperated callers offer a succession of desperate solutions to encourage a bit of singing. The last of these, a possible devotee of *Songs of Praise,* suggests the distribution of song sheets. At this stage, the embarrassed host calls time on the debate, and swiftly reaches for a travel bulletin.

It's time for us to reflect on the day's events. I'm quite satisfied with the point, but Leo and family are a bit down. They feel that they have been robbed, and they are blaming the woodwork, the ref, the scarf - you name it. It hasn't all been bad, though: they have enjoyed a quiet afternoon out in a nice peaceful environment, and have been able to read a few more chapters of their current books.

COMPANION 21

Name:	**Brian Clancy**
Birthplace:	**Hampstead, London**
Relationship:	**Brother-in-law**
Allegiance:	**Manchester United**

Relevant History

Brian is one of those sick-making, glory-hunting, southern Manchester United supporters. Geographically speaking, he should support QPR, Fulham or Chelsea, but when he first discovered the joys of football in the early 1960s, Best, Charlton and Law were in their prime, so it was no contest.

As soon as he could afford it, he was hopping on the tube to follow his heroes around the London grounds, and in that respect, he is one of the privileged few. He still holds many recollections of watching Bestie single-handedly take top sides apart, and he witnessed some breath-taking goals too; goals that are only visible in the memories of those present; goals that were never filmed by Match of the Day's selective cameras. It's a sad fact that any George Best videos that are now available on the market, can only give us a small glimpse of the man's true genius.

In the 1970s and 80s, Brian tried his luck with a few FA Cup finals. He never turned up with a ticket in his pocket, but this was apparently not a problem. All he had to do was find an enterprising steward, slip him a tenner, and Bob's your uncle. This was common practice at the big finals in this era, and attendances must have been well in excess of 100 000. It certainly makes me wonder again about the Hillsborough disaster.

In recent years, he hasn't managed to take in quite so many matches. There are two reasons for this. Firstly, he went and got married and had two kids, and secondly, he got in with a bad crowd – rugby players. His Saturday afternoons over the last twenty years have been spent playing Rugby Union for Camelot in Hemel Hempstead, even though he is far too old.

He still hasn't had the pleasure of attending a Hull City match, although I nearly dragged him along to a frozen Milton Keynes on a dark Tuesday night in February 2005. Not surprisingly, he declined the offer, but he's a lucky boy – I've given him a second chance.

VENUE 21 – BRAMALL LANE

Sheffield United 3 Hull City 2

Saturday 8th April 2006 – 3pm

Even Brian's nippy little Ford Ka is unable to squeeze into a parking spot, and after three or four fruitless circuits of a one-way system, we finally succumb to the expensive charms of a multi-story car park at the railway station. A ten-minute walk is now required, which wouldn't normally be a problem, but it's absolutely pissing down with rain. We're a bit pushed for time, so we reluctantly step out into the torrent.

Consequently, our condition on arrival at the ground, could best be described as 'damp.' We settle uncomfortably into our seats in the top tier of the Gordon Lamb Stand, right behind the goal, and drink in the Yorkshire derby atmosphere. It is an impressive showing from the Tigers fans, considering that we're now twelve points clear of relegation with just five games to play, and we almost fill the allotted area.

City have a storming start, and the Blades can't get out of their own half for at least thirty seconds. The next half an hour is more balanced, but we are still having the better of it, and we come close with two long-range efforts. Firstly, Andrews whistles one just past the post, and then Ellison forces Paddy Kenny into a great save down to his left. We are right behind the shot, and it looks for all the world as if it is heading for the bottom corner of the net, but the dumpy keeper somehow gets across to it.

Meanwhile, at the near end, Neil Shipperly is proving to be a handful for the City defence. I can't make up my mind whether he is strong and muscular, or just plain fat. It's probably a bit of both, but throw in a bit of Premiership experience, and you've got a canny striker who can be of great value to a promotion seeking side. It would certainly explain how he manages to brush Thelwell aside to flick Michael Tonge's 36th minute cross into the net.

Until this point, City had looked the better side, but now the tide seems to be turning, and the lively Danny Webber is becoming more influential. Myhill is called into action more than once before the break to keep it at 1-0.

Brian and I go for a half time stroll, but the area behind the stand is heaving with fans, and I abort my initial plan to seek out my cousin. Instead, we return to our seats and sit back to be entertained by four 5-a-side matches that have been organised in separate quarters of the pitch. Actually, 'entertained' is the wrong word, as the quality of play from the young lads is pretty dire, and we assume that they must be privileged winners of some kind of local competition to play on the hallowed Bramall Lane turf.

It's a relief when the four referees call time on the dull little kick around, but it's a surprise to learn that the youngsters on show are all from the Sheffield United academy. With the Blades seemingly destined for the Premiership, the future looks bleak for this mediocre crop of young South Yorkshire hopefuls. The financial requirement these days is for instant success, and if United are to maintain their money-spinning status in the top flight, a few ready-made stars will have to be shipped in (probably from abroad) leaving little opportunity for the academy lads to prove their worth at the top level. If retained, their most likely prospect will be a series of loans to the likes of Rotherham or Doncaster in search of regular first team football. Progress at Premiership clubs is invariably blocked nowadays for all but the cream of the crop, and even then, they'd have to be extremely creamy.

The semi-skimmed kids vacate the pitch and allow the real players back on. Within seven minutes United score a second, which is almost a carbon copy of the first. This time it is Paul Ifill who nips in front of Dawson to head home. The Tigers are looking doomed.

Taylor reacts with a double substitution. Paynter has not looked comfortable on the right of midfield, so he is withdrawn. Ellison switches wings, allowing Elliott to adopt his familiar left wing role. Up front, Duffy comes on for Fagan.

The changes have the desired effect. The Sheffield defence have not done their homework on the Elliott goal threat, and within minutes, he's ghosting in at the back post, totally unmarked, to coolly convert Thelwell's cross.

Suddenly, the Blades have got the jitters, and City are pressing for the equaliser. When Paddy Kenny clutches hold of Green's ankle instead of the ball, preventing a certain goal, it seems as if the time has come. Kenny stays down, clutching his head, hoping that a bit of sympathy might help to avert the certain red card, but incredibly, nothing is given! It's hard to believe that neither the referee or linesman have seen one of the most blatant penalties in the history of the world. I can only assume that they have bottled it, petrified by the prospect of incurring Neil Warnock's wrath after the game.

There is a brief stoppage while Kenny receives treatment from the physio, but this is nothing compared to the treatment that the City fans are giving him:

"You fat bastard, you fat bastard..."

"Kenny, Kenny, what's the score..."

He turns round and holds up the appropriate number of fingers to remind us that they are still 2-1 up.

Not for long! Elliott lofts a lovely ball to Green on the right side of the area, and his first time cross leaves Duffy with a simple tap in. Kenny gets another bang on the head for his efforts, and there is another lengthy hold up while the bald Irishman receives several more applications of the magic sponge. We ask him for another score check:

"Fat boy, fat boy, what's the score?

Fat boy, what's the score?"

This time, there is no response to the barracking, probably because the dazed keeper doesn't actually have a clue what the score is.

The Blades back four appear to have little confidence in Kenny, and shortly afterwards, Chris Morgan opts to hack clear a through-ball, which he would normally have left to the keeper. It's a bad decision. Not only does he clatter into Kenny to floor him for the third time, but he also slices the clearance straight to Stuart Elliott. He tries a first time long-range header, but it trickles wide of the empty goal.

Yet again, the medics are called onto the pitch to assess the keeper's state of consciousness. The 100% foolproof method for detecting concussion is tried, where three fingers are held up in front of the face, and the casualty has to guess how many. Kenny's eyes are all over the place and he would have trouble guessing the number of hands, let alone fingers.

It is clear to everyone that he should be removed from the fray, but there is no substitute keeper, and United can feel three valuable points slipping away. If this was a boxing contest, the referee and doctors would stop the fight, fearful of further damage, but they are more fearful of Warnock, and Kenny is allowed to continue.

He manages to avoid any further knockouts and United re-assert their authority towards the end. We expect a monumental amount of stoppage time but only five minutes are eventually added. Elliott and Dawson try to see out this period by keeping the ball near the corner flag, but they barely manage five seconds and United are able to break. We regain possession but then sloppily give it away again. Cort almost retrieves the situation but Webber steps in and releases Kabba for a clear strike at goal. He scuffs his shot, and Myhill deflects it round the post.

A mass scramble ensues from the resulting corner. Myhill makes another great point-blank save but it eventually drops to Unsworth, and he smacks it home. We are three minutes into stoppage time, and my heart goes out to hundreds of Tigers fans around the country that are following this on Teletext or Final Score. At this very moment, they will be watching the clock as it ticks past 4.50pm, certain that the game will be over; daring to believe that we have pulled off a creditable 2-2 draw against promotion candidates. But, the bad news is about to flash up on the screen – *Unsworth 90*.

Their guts will twist, the curses will flow, and they will kick the nearest piece of furniture, or an innocent child, or the cat (which is probably guilty of something).

Yet somehow, as I sit watching pandemonium break out all over Bramall Lane, I find myself being quite philosophical about the Blades' late winner. After all, we are safe from relegation, we certainly can't make the play-offs, and we've just given a mighty fright to a side that will grace the Premiership next season. The sinking feeling was ten times worse last month at Leicester when the late winner seemed like the end of the world.

The referee calls time and the celebrations continue for the home fans. The three points must feel like six, as Watford and Leeds both fail to win. Paddy Kenny has regained his senses and he turns to the City fans with his arms aloft. This provokes an angry reaction from three or four plonkers, who can dish it out, but can't take it. They try to invade the pitch to give Kenny some close-up abuse, but they are unceremoniously bundled away by the police, and quite rightly so.

As a neutral, Brian feels that Kenny is fully entitled to have a little gloat. His second half antics, and the ongoing banter with the crowd have helped to bring the game to life, and despite the defeat, it has to go down as one of the matches of the season.

It is suggested after the game that Kenny might find himself in hot water for stirring things up, but Neil Warnock puts it all in perspective with the quote of the season:

"If Paddy Kenny gets reported to the Football League for inciting the crowd, then I'll report two thousand Hull fans for calling him a fat bastard."

Fair enough.

VENUE 22 – THE KC STADIUM

Hull City 0 Burnley 0

Saturday 15th April 2006 – 3pm

It had to happen. It's only fair. How could I possibly omit the K.C. Stadium from my nationwide analysis of Championship grounds? It would leave the survey incomplete, and neutral readers would be forever wondering how my hometown facilities compare with the rest of the division.

A recent fans' survey in *Four Four Two* Magazine, rated the K.C. as the best Championship stadium to visit, so it is only natural that I should assess the ground from the away fans' perspective. For one day only, therefore, I shall infiltrate the North Stand, and become a Burnley fan.

In a true test of friendship and loyalty, my old school pal, Dave (see Companion 10) has agreed to tag along to lend some moral support. This slightly complicates the undercover operation as it doubles the risk of detection. We're unlikely to last the ninety minutes without talking, but the opposition are northerners, so we should get away with it.

Any fan, tiger or not, cannot fail to be bowled over by their first sighting of our fine new stadium. Today, we approach from the east, crossing the railway bridge near the Hull Royal Infirmary. The grand West Stand peeps out above the smaller East Stand, giving a tantalising glimpse of the impressive interior. Hordes of fans are following the long concrete path towards the great temple, and there is a tangible buzz of excitement, even though the season is effectively over for both sides. Price concessions have been introduced for the run-in, and another crowd of over 20 000 is expected.

We reach the steep steps at the end of the trail. It is time for us to part company with Dave's two young sons, Joseph and Adam, and his next-door neighbour, Sean. Dave has found it hard to explain to his children why Daddy is defecting to the other side today. Sean understands, but he still thinks that we're mad, and he's convinced that Dave will get us thrown out with his animated reactions.

I've been in the wrong end at away grounds before, but it feels really strange to be queuing up with Burnley fans on our home patch. I can't help feeling conspicuous, and I try to avoid making eye contact with stewards and police. In fact, I try to avoid making contact of any sort, with anyone, even Dave.

We eventually pay our way in without speaking, and climb the stairs to a spacious area at the back of the North Stand containing several food outlets. There are more than enough TV screens bracketed to the walls, keeping us abreast of the early kick-offs, and there's even a small hatch where forgetful fans can buy their programme. Nice touch.

Our next task is to find a seat, preferably away from the main bulk of Burnley fans, but the police have neatly packaged us all into a tight space, so we end up in the thick of it. The surroundings take on an unfamiliar appearance from this alien position. The two-tiered West Stand is now on our right, and City fans surround us on all three sides. It doesn't feel like we are in the K.C.

In order to keep up our pretence, Dave and I decide to join in with the singing, and we find ourselves pointing across at the East Stand during the pre-match introductions chanting, "Who are ya, who are ya..."

For the next number, we learn that singing the name of the Lancastrian outfit is more complicated than we first thought. They've adopted an idea traditionally used by Eng-er-land fans, and Burnley now has three syllables in it: "Burn-er-ley, Burn-er-ley, Burn-er-ley..."

An excellent atmosphere is being generated as the two sets of fans compete to out sing each other. It beats me where all these noisy Burnley folk were hiding at Turf Moor last October – the quietest ground on my nine-month tour. In contrast, the East Stand of the K.C. are giving a very good account of themselves and must rate as one of the most vocal sets of home fans so far encountered.

The game kicks off, so Dave and I sit on our hands, bite our lips and clench our buttocks. One false yelp now, and we'll be frogmarched out. There is plenty of chatter around us, though, and we are initially confused by several shouts of encouragement for the Beast. It turns out that this is also the nickname of their giant goalkeeper, Brian Jensen. He's a big bugger, and our lightweight striker, Darryl Duffy needs to be careful. If he gets sandwiched between Jensen and Parkin, it could create quite a mess.

An irritating double act behind us have got an awful lot to say, and it is obvious already that we'll have to put up with their running commentaries until at least half time, when a tactical move will be necessary. With their strong Lancastrian accents, they sound a lot like Cannon and Ball, and their over-critical opinions have singled out Graham Branch as today's scapegoat. Burnley's longest serving player is having a bit of a mare, and every stray pass is greeted with cries of, "Oh Branchy, what ya doin' Branchy." Thankfully, Burnley's best chance of the half falls to him, but he drags his shot across the goal, and we feel confident enough to join in with the general condemnation: "Oh Branchy, what was that Branchy!"

City's best chance falls to Ellison at the back post from Thelwell's cross, but instead of sweeping it into the net, he miscues, and the ball trickles into Jensen's arms.

At half time we go for a wander, and take the chance to warm up a bit. It's a nice day, but a cool breeze has chilled us to the bone in the shady North Stand. On our return, we reluctantly decide to stick with the same seats, in front of Cannon and Ball, as very few others appear to be available. Cannon is now obsessed with the large number of adverts for DeVries Honda in the West Stand. Ball helps him to count, and they decide that there are eleven placards. They are absolutely amazed by this: eleven signs, for one company, all in the same stand? It has clearly escaped their attention that DeVries Honda sponsors the West Stand. That's why it is called the 'DeVries Honda West Stand.' It is really tempting to turn round and point out this painfully obvious fact, but Dave holds me back.

The second half develops into the most boring 45 minutes of football ever. Chances are at a premium, and the few that are created fly tamely at the keepers. The inactivity on the pitch at least negates the threat of Dave leaping up to blow our cover, and it would take an extremely vigilant steward to detect our low level sighs and tuts as a series of City attacks break down.

We amuse ourselves by slating Branchy every time he receives a touch, although we could be tempting fate here, and we worry that he may end up scoring the winner. It's a relief when the final whistle releases us from the boredom, although we're not exactly free to go. The police guide us towards the Burnley coaches, and we begin to fret that a surprise trip across the Pennines may be in the offing. There is no escape. A large set of iron gates remain firmly padlocked, and it is clear that we will be staying put until those troublesome Hull fans have cleared the area. This is the only time all season that I have been penned in after the match. How ironic that it should be at my home ground, alongside an opposing set of supporters.

After a frustrating fifteen-minute wait, the police finally decide that the coast is clear and we are set free. It has been an instantly forgettable match for all but two of the crowd. Dave and I will at least remember it as the day that we became Burn-er-ley fans.

COMPANIONS 22 &23

Names: **Hugh & Michele McAllister**
Birthplace: **Hull**
Relationship: **Cousin & his wife (cousin-in-law?)**
Allegiance: **Hull City**

Relevant History

Hugh

If I ever felt the urge for a game of footy in my childhood, I knew that I could just nip across the street with my brothers to the Oak Road Playing Fields. The central field was very much the stronghold of the lads from Etherington Road (that's us) but if we ever yearned to test our skills against foreign opposition, we could always head south into the next field to take on the Etherington Drive gang. A short foray to the north would take us into Riversdale Road territory.

We would always observe the Oak Road etiquette by approaching potential opponents with the question:

"Are you larkin'?"

If an enjoyable sporting contest ensued, they would be classified as 'good larkers' and we would keep them in mind for future battles.

On some visits, there was a distinct lack of bodies on these three fields, and we were forced to venture into a fourth field, crossing the boundary into Beresford Park. Here, we would invariably come across our cousins: John, Hugh and Damien, kicking around with a selection of 'good larkers' from the Beresford, Wellesley and Ormond regions.

Hugh was probably one of the biggest football fanatics that I knew. He always seemed to have a ball under his arm or at his feet, and he talked, slept and ate football, especially anything to do with Hull City. He was always at Boothferry Park, and we would usually come across him at some point during every game. Often, we would stand half way up the terrace in Bunkers' but if there was a big crowd, we would move down to the front so that we could see the action.

This policy was reviewed after the 1973 FA Cup encounter with Bobby Moore's West Ham United, when a large proportion of the 32 000 crowd rolled forward to crush young Hugh against the front barrier. At the time, I thought that it was the excitement of Ken Houghton's goal that made Hugh faint, but apparently, it was just a straightforward case of oxygen starvation. The St. John's ambulance people were called into action and Hugh was stretchered away, never to be seen again: well, not until the following day anyway. He was kept under observation for the rest of the match and missed the conclusion, a giant-killing 1-0 win.

In later years, after marriage and children, he graduated to the relative safety of the family enclosure in the West Stand, where I would always dutifully give his kids a cheery little wave before the game.

Since moving to the KC, his family have secured a wonderful spot above an exit in the West Stand, where no one can sit in front and block their view. I expect them to hold onto these seats for a number of seasons, from where they can happily cheer on their favourite larkers.

Michele

It has dawned on me recently, that all of my closest friends are passionate about football. I have always found it very hard to identify with non-sporty types and it can be a real challenge to maintain a lengthy and meaningful conversation.

In my youth, this meant that I found it very difficult to chat to girls. Statistically, only a small percentage of females develop the same genuine passion and in-depth knowledge about the game, so it must be a colossal bonus for anyone who is able to court and marry a real live female fanatic.

Hugh landed on his feet in this respect, and Michele has clearly been the perfect partner for him. Not only is she a keen follower of the beautiful game, but she is potty about the Tigers as well.

I found this hard to believe when I first met her, and I was particularly suspicious of her maiden name – Barnsley. Surely, she would harbour secret affections for the South Yorkshire club, and would be unable to resist looking out for their score each week, in the same way that I look out for Paul Collingwood's cricket score.

Another nagging doubt was provided by the identity of her favourite ever player: not Wagstaff, Chilton or Pearson, but Allan Clarke! Yes, that's right, grumpy old Sniffer Clarke from Don Revie's ruthless Leeds United side of the early 1970s.

These two concerns combined in 1978 when Allan Clarke worryingly became the manager of Barnsley. Once again, I fretted that she would rather be a Tyke than a Tiger, but twenty-eight years on, I accept that she does indeed have the amber blood of Hull City running through her veins, rather than the red of Barnsley.

She has been a season ticket holder since the 1970s and has successfully managed to bring up her two sons to enjoy the same healthy obsession.

VENUE 23 – PRIDE PARK

Derby County 1 Hull City 1

Monday 17th April 2006 – 3pm

The first official double act on my list arrives at 11am ready for an early getaway, but they are immediately seduced by my Mum's irresistible cream cakes and cheese scones. We settle down for a quick coffee, while in time-honoured fashion, Mum checks that we're all wearing enough layers of clothing to stop us from catching a chill. She is particularly concerned by Michele's thin black Tigers replica top. Once again, my mother has forgotten that we are all now in our forties.

The coffee and cakes are going down very well, but the clock on the front room mantelpiece is ticking away, and it is gone midday before we finally hit the road.

My family have all spent the Easter weekend in Hull and they are going to drive back to Hemel Hempstead without me. This shouldn't be a problem, so long as my cunning little plan pays off. I have purchased an extra ticket for Vin, an old school friend who lives in Hampshire. We hope to link up with him outside the ground, and then he can lift me back to Hertfordshire after the game.

Hugh is in the driving seat, and we get to Derbyshire without a hitch. Pride Park is situated in the middle of a new industrial estate and retail park, and we arrive early enough to go in search of food. Hugh is keen to try out the pies inside the ground, but we can't go in until we've met up with Vin – we've got his ticket.

A number of classy eating establishments await our custom. It basically boils down to a choice between Burger King, KFC and Pizza Hut. We plump for Burger King on the supposition that it will be quicker.

Just as I'm polishing off my last French fry, Vin phones to inform me that he's stuck in a jam on the M1 and will almost certainly fail to make the kick off. That wasn't in the plan. I assure him that we will seek advice at the stadium, and will phone back with an update.

True to our word, we reach turnstile 55 and explain the problem to a steward. He points to a great big solid iron door next to the turnstile, with a large letter 'W' above it. He recommends that we enter the ground, and leave the ticket with the steward who should be standing behind it. Apparently, entrance 'W' will be opened up shortly after kick off, and all that Vin will have to do is present himself to the correct steward. Sounds simple!

We do as we are told and the dilemma is re-explained to the man behind the door, where I trustingly hand over the ticket. He takes down Vin's particulars and promises us that all will be well, although the smirk on his face gives me a slight feeling of unease.

I phone the instructions through to Vin, and he sounds similarly anxious, but there's not much we can do now apart from keep our fingers crossed. Michele, Hugh and I now focus on the football and we make it to our seats behind the goal, where the view is not unlike that experienced from the South Stand of the K.C. Stadium. To our left, we have a large two-tiered stand with private boxes half way up. The rest of the ground does not rise to the same height and consists of one large tier, although strangely, our match tickets claim that we are sitting in an upper tier. Presumably, the narrow gangway across the middle is the dividing line. The main distinctive feature is a grey concrete section in the far left corner, which houses a few more executive boxes and a scoreboard.

Both sets of fans are lively and a good atmosphere is building. Derby line up in their familiar white tops, City are in black, and the match officials are wearing black and amber, which is most encouraging.

Craig Fagan seems very sharp early on, and he looks as if he's really up for this one. Derby's only chance of note comes from a Peschisolido snapshot, which flies well over.

After fifteen minutes, a familiar figure appears further along our row. It's Vin. I'd forgotten all about him. He has picked up his ticket at gate 'W' without a problem, and because of his bad time keeping, a kind official has even allowed him to park his car in a 'permit holders only' space. It has already started to play on Vin's mind, though, that the official didn't look very official, and it's possible that he has been the victim of a practical joke. Still, we'll worry about that after the game.

Two minutes after taking his seat, Vin decides that Scott Wiseman is not playing very well, which is a bit harsh, as he's only just walked in.

Young Scott has actually had a good opening to the game, nullifying the threat of Lee Holmes on the left flank.

After 33 minutes, City take the lead with an absolute wonder strike. Stuart Green is making a late bid to become our leading scorer, which let's face it, shouldn't be too hard this season – he only needs seven! His volley sears into the top corner, and he follows it with a ninety-yard sprint towards the City fans, where he's saved just about enough energy for a brief celebration.

Over in the far corner, the scoreboard illuminates the state of play: *Derby County 0 Hull City 1*.

Directly above it, the slogan for a local insurance company reads, "How fair is that?"

Spot on!

At half time, Michele nips out to the toilet, and on her return, she files a detailed report. Thanks to this, I can now state with complete confidence that the Ladies' facilities at Pride Park are amongst the best in the division. Apparently, they have got mirrors, and this is what makes the difference. It has enabled Michele to re-apply her make-up and brush her hair. I just hope the players appreciate the effort that she is making.

City's strikers toil to make some headway after the break, and Jon Parkin is becoming particularly frustrated. The smaller Derby players keep bouncing off him, but they seem to be winning free kicks for this. Eventually, the Beast acts out a mime to the referee as if he is pumping iron, the inference being that they all need to work out more.

A worrying little spell then follows, where City keep giving away possession, and Derby are able to gain the upper hand. It feels as if the equaliser is on its way, but then the balance of power swings suddenly back towards City, and we create three excellent chances.

Firstly, the hyperactive Fagan bursts down the left, and chips a superb cross to the far post, where Parkin's goal bound volley deflects to safety off the arse of a fortunate defender.

Next, Stuart Green, who is still striving for the top scorer accolade, tries his luck again from distance, but it is tipped over by Derby's impressive England Under 21 keeper, who is camp – no really, that's his name – Lee Camp.

Leon Cort then has a trademark header cleared off the line, but it remains 1-0, and we brace ourselves for the tension of Derby's final onslaught.

Tommy Smith has switched to the left, and Derby's latest ploy, is to spray the ball out to his touchline. It proves to be quite effective, as Wiseman now looks tired and disorientated. Hugh tells me that a friend of a friend of a friend spoke to a Hull City insider, who revealed that Wiseman is known within the club as a 'speedboat without a driver.' Well, it's definitely a case of 'man overboard' in the final minutes, as Smith repeatedly creates problems for him down the wing.

The pressure eventually tells with a minute left, when he concedes a penalty. From a distance, it looks pretty innocuous, but the referee manages to spot a minor push. Clearly, his black and amber top has not engendered a sub-conscious leaning towards the Tigers.

Tommy Smith (incidentally, a native of Hemel Hempstead and a former pupil at my wife's school) steps up to convert the kick. Yet again, we have conceded a late goal. That's six times in the last twelve matches, and it's a habit that we will have to shake off if we're to taste life in the top half of the table next season.

The feeling is the same as at Sheffield United last week. I'm disappointed with the late goal, but it won't ruin my Easter holiday. Once safety was procured, these end of season games lost their edge, and I'm now becoming a little blasé. I'm almost wishing that we desperately needed the points…almost: not quite, but almost!

There is no clamp on Vin's car, so we quickly aim for the M1 to join the London-bound bank holiday traffic. Michele and Hugh go north. No doubt, I will see them at the KC for an early season fixture in August.

COMPANION 24

Name: Nick Baker
Birthplace: Watford
Relationship: Work colleague
Allegiance: Watford

Relevant History

In October 2000, Nick had duped me into watching a 'Manchester United XI' turn out for an insignificant Worthington Cup tie at Watford. We were due to rendezvous at my house at five o'clock, but it had been a hectic day; I was stressed, and I was running late. As I drove home past a stream of dazzling headlights, I gradually became aware of the onset of an untimely migraine. The vision on my right side was becoming blurred, and a sizeable blind spot was developing, dangerously shielding my view of oncoming traffic. I should have pulled over really, but I chose to rely on a combination of great skill and complete guesswork. The consequences of meeting an identical migraine sufferer driving in the opposite direction could have been disastrous, but somehow, I made it safely home without clipping any bollards, lampposts or pedestrians.

An excited Nick was already waiting for me, so I grabbed a quick sandwich, downed four paracetamol, and off we went. Nick was driving so I was able to relax and dream of all the top European stars that I would soon be watching. The tablets appeared to be having the desired effect and all the psychedelic patterns began to subside. Normal service would be resumed to my picture in time for kick off.

I probably was not the only member of the crowd who felt a tad cheated when the Red Devil's team sheet was read out. A mixture of little known reserves and juniors were reeled off, and the only player with a genuine claim for first team status was Ole Gunnar Solskjaer (or Solskjaera, as Barry Davies insisted on pronouncing it), and Ole's notoriety was founded on being a decent substitute.

The 'contest' had the air of a practice match, and the £16 that I had stumped up for the ticket seemed mightily overpriced when compared to the entertainment on offer. Solskjaer's inclusion was clearly designed to provide the team of nobodies with a cutting edge, and the plan worked perfectly. He scored twice, and then Dwight Yorke (a laid-back second half substitute) notched the third. Watford were never in it and the game fizzled out. Hordes of Hornets fans left early, depressed by the knowledge that their beloved side would even struggle in the Pontins League.

Nick owed me one, so when the Tigers produced an incredible second half to the season, (despite being paid no wages), and forced their way into the play-offs, he was presented with a chance to repay his debt. We were paired with Orient in the semi-final and John Eyre gave us a slender advantage from the first leg at Boothferry Park to leave it finely balanced. Nick agreed to come to the second leg, and then converted his debt into overflowing credit by informing me that he could wangle some free tickets. His brother's friend was a football agent and some of the Orient players were on his books. Nick seemed confident that his brother could deliver, but it didn't sound very convincing when I explained to people that my ticket was coming via the 'friend of a brother of a friend'.

It is probably a safe assumption, that when Nick agreed to come along, he was blissfully unaware of the clash with the UEFA Cup Final. The 2001 showpiece between Liverpool and Alaves turned out to be a nine-goal classic, and over the course of the evening, he was to become increasingly conscious of the folly of his rash decision to check out the Tigers.

My only concern in the hours leading up to kick off was the whereabouts of my complimentary ticket. Nick had agreed, over his mobile, to meet the agent outside the ground but when we arrived at the prearranged meeting point, there was no sign of him. Nick got back on his mobile. Eventually, he got through and discovered that the 'special agent' was inside the ground, supping drinks, and generally enjoying

'Oriental' hospitality, but crucially, he did have our tickets and would be appearing outside shortly.

Within seconds, a gum-chewing hard man, with a husky cockney accent and piercing blue eyes appeared by Nick's side and pulled out a bundle of tickets from his trench coat. He made no eye contact, so I escaped getting a piercing from his gaze. He seemed a little preoccupied, and nervously glanced from left to right along the street. Now where had I seen that look before? Oh yes, Rodney and Del-Boy, when stationed on a street corner, flogging a suitcase full of dodgy goods. He thumbed through his little stash, removed two tickets and passed them to Nick. He then disappeared into the night, as quickly as he had arrived, presumably to go and finish his nibbles and champagne – lovely jubbly. I immediately dragged Nick off towards the Hull end, not a hundred percent convinced that our tickets were kosher.

We passed through the turnstiles without a hitch and took up our position behind the goal, just in time. City were attacking towards the far end, although I use the term 'attacking' loosely, as it was clear from the outset, that we were already settling for the 0-0 that would see us through to the Millennium Stadium. Orient were doing most of the probing, but the Tigers defence looked sound. About twenty minutes into the drab stalemate, Nick received a text-alert: 2-0 to Liverpool – Gerard. I knew what he was thinking. For the next ten minutes, we said very little; there certainly wasn't a lot to talk about on the pitch. Nick's phone went off again: 3-1 to Liverpool – McAllister – penalty. The look on his face now left me in no doubt whatsoever as to what he was thinking.

The game before us continued in the same vein as before, and City were looking pretty ineffective up front. John Eyre was very subdued and he received little help from his '6 foot, 7 inch' carthorse of a partner, Kevin Francis. I can't quite remember where we signed Francis from: was it Stockport County or the Harlem Globetrotters? We never really looked like scoring, although the giant striker did try a couple of hopeful long pots. He was still clearly under the impression that goals from outside the area counted as three pointers. On the stroke of half time, Francis provided us with further evidence of his greater suitability for basketball. A promising City move was abruptly ended when big Kev trod on the ball and fell flat on his arse. Orient instantly took advantage by counter attacking and finding the net to bring the scores level on aggregate.

Brian Little's second half tactic appeared to be the same as the first, except we were now playing for penalties instead. So, Little changed little, and Orient still looked the more likely. Another text alert – 3-3.

"Blimey Nick, that's some game we're missing!"

Silence.

Then – disaster. The Orient full back, Matt Lockwood, scored the goal of his career, a sublime left-footed strike that swerved into the top corner. Now, one might have reasonably expected the Tigers to come out of their shells at this point and launch an 'all or nothing' assault on the Orient goal. But no, we continued to offer no threat, and only one looping header from Mark Greaves stretched their keeper. A dark gloom descended on the City end, whilst in the Orient ranks, it was carnival time and the air was filled with songs about being on their way to Cardiff. Just to rub salt into the wounds, Nick's phone piped up again: 4-3 to Liverpool – Fowler. This time, Nick told me what he was thinking.

We exited the ground and I swiftly found a pub in order to placate Nick with a couple of beers. The television in the corner appeared to be showing highlights of the UEFA Final, but on closer inspection, we realised that the score was now 4-4 and it had gone into extra time. Nick now looked more cheerful and he was further appeased when I fought my way back from the bar to thrust a cold pint of lager into his hand.

Alaves had gone down to ten men and were trying all the tricks in the book to waste time and make it to penalties. Then, Smicer got rugby tackled, and they were down to nine. McAllister's resultant free-kick deflected off an Alaves head to provide Liverpool with the golden goal, and the trophy. Our spirits were now raised as we watched Fowler and Hyypia jointly raise the UEFA Cup, and I was momentarily able to put City's lacklustre display out of my mind.

It doesn't seem to matter what is on the television when you are sitting in a pub; you are unable to deflect your eyes for long from the screen. Consequently, most of the gathering continued to gawp towards the corner of the room as the BBC News followed the football. The opening titles on this particular evening were relaying pictures of the famous egg-throwing incident involving our esteemed Deputy Prime-Minister, Mr. John Prescott. His reaction to the point blank attack did not follow political protocol; he preferred instead to rely on the Hull protocol of, beating the shit out of his aggressor. Great cheers rang out around the pub as all the Tigers fans came back to life, and a chorus of song broke out to the tune of the 'Can-Can'...

"Nah, nah, nah, nah. He's from Hull and he's from Hull..."

As we departed, and headed back to my car, I allowed myself to dwell on the beautiful thought that Prescott's shocked attacker might have been an Orient fan.

VENUE 24 – VICARAGE ROAD

Watford 0 Hull City 0

Sunday 30th April 2006 – 1.30pm

In the words of Alanis Morissette, "Isn't it Ironic?"

After my extensive travels around the country, the final fixture of the season is right on my doorstep, five miles down the road in Watford. At least I know where I'm going to park. The Harlequin Shopping Centre is a familiar haunt, and my car knows the way by itself.

Nick has decided that we should meet at the *Moon Under Water*. I'm not sure if this is the name of a pub, or secret code for some kind of local beauty spot. Either way, it is apparently on the High Street, so I wander up and down until I find it. I'm a bit early, so I nip into Woolworths, opposite, to stock up on sweets.

A big packet of Maltesers later, Nick finally arrives, having dropped his wife and baby off at the Harlequin. The arrangement seems to be that he can go to the football, while they run amok with the credit cards. It could prove to be an expensive day.

He is not wearing his Watford colours, and it's just as well. The pub is a Hull stronghold, and Tigers are outnumbering Hornets by 2 to 1, not that this represents any serious threat to Nick's health. I have come to realise over the course of the season, that the chances of encountering a fight are about as likely as seeing a Craig Fagan hat-trick.

We head for the bar and sink a couple of quiet beers while I bore him with tales of my travels around the other 23 grounds. He retaliates with enthusiastic talk of Aidy Boothroyd's inspirational qualities, Watford's chances in the play-offs, and the state of his son's nappies.

Vicarage Road is only a short walk away, and we are soon queuing up outside the imaginatively named Vicarage Road Stand. Nick has gallantly agreed to sit in the City end, although I'm sure he wouldn't have been so keen if this game had been in any way important. As it stands, a draw will guarantee Watford third place, but they'll still be in the play-offs, regardless.

City have made just the one change from last week's home draw with Preston. Thelwell has replaced Wiseman at right back, and he is looking very sharp in the early stages as he repeatedly snuffs out the left wing threat of the highly rated Ashley Young. Just as I am thinking how fit and strong Thelwell is looking, Nick observes that Young is looking tired and sluggish – it's probably a bit of both.

It's not a bad old place that Watford have, but they will need to pay attention to the bitty East Stand if Premiership football comes calling. It looks like an amalgamation of remnant pieces from other defunct grounds, and consists of four main parts.

Nearest to us, we have an area of crumbling redundant terracing. Then, we get a small area of uncovered seating. The third section, in the centre, holds about two thousand seats, but the top half has been condemned, rendering the roof useless, as the decent seats at the front are open to the elements. Finally, there is another section of seating at the far end with a higher roof. According to Nick, this area has always been known as the Neutral Stand: as if thousands of neutrals would bother to watch Watford each week.

Not much sound is coming from the Rookery, directly opposite, where the noisiest Watford fans are meant to dwell. Nick tries hard to convince me that this is due to poor acoustics, and he insists that they're probably singing but we just can't hear them. He has no explanation, though, for the complete lack of movement from the statuesque crowd.

The City fans tire of enticing them into song and start up a singing contest of their own. Just behind us, a small contingent bursts into song:

"Left side, left side, give us a song…"

The left side of the City end obliges, and they reply with:

"Left side Tigers…" setting off a chain reaction.

"Right side Tigers."

"Left side Tigers."

"Right side Tigers," and so on…

This is all quite amusing to begin with, but by half time, the joke has worn thin, and they've become a complete pain in the arse. Not a lot has happened on the pitch to keep our minds off it. Green has produced our best effort, bringing a good save out of Foster, and Chris Eagles has displayed his Manchester United credentials with a twisting run, which required a reflex save from Myhill's right foot.

The Tigers take the field for the second half with Duffy having replaced Fagan, and it doesn't take him long to get into the action. He drags one shot wide after being set up by Parkin, then has another well saved by Foster after being fed by Green.

It takes a while for Watford to threaten, but towards the end, they do. Myhill makes another stop with his feet to deny 19-year-old Alhassan Bangura. Now *there's* an interesting story. Six years ago, Bangura was fleeing from gun-touting rebels on the poverty-stricken streets of Sierra Leone. He initially escaped to France, but it was 'out of the frying pan and into the fire.' His French guardian was a pimp who tried to exploit him as a rent boy! He escaped again, this time to England, where he started playing football for non-league Chertsey. Watford scouts soon spotted him and he rapidly rose from academy hopeful to first team regular. Now, it is a different kind of 'tackle from behind' that Al needs to watch out for.

The young African is unable to find a way through the Tigers defence, and as the clock runs down, the Hornets appear to be settling for the point, which secures third place in the Championship and a play-off semi-final tie with Crystal Palace.

I'm interested to know from Nick, the key areas that will need strengthening if they are promoted. He ponders for a moment. "All over really."

On the walk back towards the shopping centre, I feel quite empty. The season is over, and my challenge has been successfully completed, but there is a real feeling of anti-climax. What the hell am I going to do for the next six weeks until the World Cup begins?

In the Harlequin, Nick phones his wife. She is in John Lewis', which is a potentially expensive situation. He says his goodbyes quickly and dashes off to put the brakes on her spending spree.

I amble forlornly back to Level 3 of the car park to begin the journey home, which is no worse than the usual trip back from a Saturday shopping expedition; a trip that I'll probably be doing every Saturday for the next fifteen weeks. My wife, Patsy, has made many sacrifices since last August, and as she keeps reminding me, "It's payback time!"

I don't know what I was worried about. The long list of potential stumbling blocks never materialised. Trains were on time, roads were relatively clear, there was no conflict with work commitments, I stayed healthy, and the aliens didn't invade; at least, not on a match day.

The biggest obstacle turned out to be my own reluctance to vacate the pubs in time for kick off. This did mean that I missed some of the opening exchanges, and regretfully, one goal: Stuart Elliott's opener at Brighton.

The long drives back from midweek games at Norwich and Preston were undoubtedly the low points and on these occasions I was forced to seriously question my own sanity. My family have questioned it a few times recently as well.

I thoroughly enjoyed surveying all of the Championship grounds, and I would have to choose Hillsborough as my overall favourite. It was just so big.

My favourite match of the season was at Stoke. It's not too often that you see City win 3-0 away from home. This game also includes my favourite goal, Jon Parkin's majestic turn and strike that put us 2-0 up. Not only was it a great piece of skill, but the timing was spot on too, coming just after Myhill had saved his first penalty, and trouble had broken out in the Stoke end.

The Stoke match was the only game where I saw anything resembling a fight. For me, this has been the most striking feature of the season, the fact that you can wear your colours with pride around rival city centres, without fear of a good kicking.

Attendances are up, and this is directly linked to the lack of trouble. An away match presents an ideal opportunity for a family day out, and I have noted a significant increase in the numbers of travelling women and children. The Tigers are now averaging nearly 20 000 for home games, compared with just 6 000 when we last played at this level in the mid-eighties.

On the pitch, it has to rate as a successful campaign. We comfortably avoided relegation by ten points, we only lost once in our last nine games, and we have established ourselves as a solid Championship side. On my travels, I witnessed four victories and eight draws, which is not bad. If we had shown some consistent home form, we could have been up near the play offs. Coventry's away record was the same as ours and they finished eighth.

So what of the future? Well, one thing is for sure, it will be without Peter Taylor, but we must never forget what he has achieved for the club. He accomplished his aims and delivered back-to-back promotions. Not too many City fans could truly have expected such instant success when he took the reins in 2002; we have all seen too many false dawns to be so foolishly wishful.

I would like to take this opportunity to personally thank Mr.Taylor for the most successful period in the club's history, but more importantly, I would like to thank him for waving to the fans every single time that we sang:

"Taylor, Taylor, give us a wave…"

He has left the club in a strong position, and let's hope that he receives a warm reception when he returns with Crystal Palace. Let us also hope that Phil Parkinson can build on the Taylor era and take us higher than we have ever been before. With Adam Pearson at the helm, I am confident that this can happen.

So, in conclusion, I hereby declare that my project has been a rip-roaring success. I made it to all 24 Championship grounds; the Tigers are now a respected side at this level, and my marriage has remained in tact.

I urge all of you home birds to get out there and explore some brand new stadia. Make a day of it, and don't forget to bring a friend!